Advance Praise for Playborhood

"*Playborhood* is important reading and an inspiration for all of us concerned with how childhood has changed."
— Po Bronson, co-author of *Nurture Shock: New Thinking About Children*

"The value of unstructured outdoor play, fading in the virtual age, is vital for children's health and happiness. This invaluable book, *Playborhood*, will inspire you create the kind of outdoor environment that nurtures the hearts of children – and parents."
— Richard Louv, author of *The Last Child in the Woods*

"While there is an increasing amount of literature bemoaning our country's growing play deficit and community apathy, Mike Lanza has decided to do something about it. This book is bursting with practical inspiration on how to transform your block into a vibrant, communal space for kids to play. His case studies span inner cities, suburbs, and small towns alike, demonstrating that no matter where you live, you have the tools in hand to effect real, lasting change for your neighborhood's youngest residents. A must-read for any parent who wants to give their kids the same kind of childhood we enjoyed -- back when outdoor play was as simple as opening the front door."
— Darell Hammond, author of *KaBOOM! How One Man Built a Movement to Save Play*

"Want to be part of a revolution that can return free outdoor play--once the birthright of childhood--to today's kids? *Playborhood* is a seriously subversive book, an inspiring "how-to" guide. It outlines with zest and clarity approaches that parents in affluent suburbs or tough inner city blocks can take to create a safe space for shared, imaginative, vigorous outdoor play that kids will love and make their own."
— Alice McLerran, author of *Roxaboxen*

"A cultu...   **EUR** ... responsible, creative
adults. S ... ...e or structured activities are a ... importance of families
engaging ... eryone."
 film, *Race to Nowhere*

"Play and love are the most formative forces for good and survival in our species' long term adventures on this planet. Good and credible neuroscience and a wealth of paleo-anthroplogic data now confirm that our 'pursuit of happiness' rests on these two elements that are foundational for our becoming fully human. What Mike Lanza accomplishes in *Playborhood* is to bring his own deep love of his kids, and his transformative knowledge of play into mainstream action, where it is most relevant and needed. The examples in the book of successful play based neighborhood activities in a wide variety of settings also confirms the power of play to bind latent community energies into a contagious pervasive play ethic. The positive implications of this readable and engaging book impact parenting, education and the building of a trusting, life-sustaining neighborhood."

— Stuart Brown MD, Founder and President of The National Institute for Play

"*Playborhood* demonstrates how we can transcend the isolation of our neighborhoods to find engagement with others. Mike Lanza gives an intuitive sense for how to do this because he and the others he writes about are 'walking the walk.' This book is full of tangible steps we can take in our neighborhoods to immediately improve our happiness, health, and sense of place."

— Fred Kent, President of the Project for Public Spaces

"*Playborhood* is the new owner's manual for your block. Everything you need to transform your neighborhood into a healthy, playful, and lively place for children and families. Reclaim your streets, trees, and front lawns – it's time to make space for free-ranging play. Mike Lanza has written the how-to manual for a new generation of families that want to do more living where they live."

— Gever Tulley, author of *50 Dangerous Things (You Should Let Your Children Do)*

"When I speak to groups of parents about the great value of children's self-directed outdoor play, the first question I'm usually asked is about how to make such play possible in today's world. My answer to date has generally begun with a reference to Mike Lanza's Playborhood website. Now I can refer them to this book! This is not only a great resource; it's also a great read. You'll enjoy it, and it'll get you thinking, even if you don't have kids. A better place for kids is a better place for all of us."

— Peter Gray, research professor and play specialist, Boston College

"In your hands is a book that is a revelation. It will teach you to see the the true meaning of the neighborhood where you live. Mike Lanza helps you honor your children's wonder of the world around them and inspires you with his strategies, vision, and community love stories."

— Mark Lakeman, founder of the City Repair Project

"When I was young my friends and I played all over our neighborhood. It was our world, and it gave us the security to go out later and explore the wider world around us. Life is different now. You can drive through the safest neighborhoods and they look like ghost towns. Not a single child is outside playing. I am so grateful to Mike Lanza for reminding us that play begins at home and in our neighborhoods. It takes so little to make it happen there – just awareness, passion, and commitment. This book helps to feed all of those."

— Joan Almon, Director, Alliance for Childhood

"In *Playborhood*, Mike Lanza reminds us that 'Go outside and play!' isn't about driving our kids away, but about enriching their lives. Even better, he lays out a wide range of examples to inspire each of us to create play-friendly spaces in our homes and blocks. Playborhood makes me want to go out and turn my front yard into the funnest place in town for kids to hang out!"

— Ken Denmead, author of the *Geek Dad* series of books

"At one level *Playborhood* is a compelling parenting guide. Mike Lanza is one of a growing number of activist parents who want their kids to have a happy childhood, acquire basic life skills, successfully navigate adolescence, and become self-reliant, socially adept, creative, problem-solving adults. In short, he proposes a return to the historic basics of healthy, happy childhoods. The Lanza key to success is for parents to take actions in the 'front space' of homes, streets, and neighborhoods.

On another level, this well-researched, lively, easy-to-read, 'Jane Jacobs primer for kids' presents timely lessons to all those who influence the spatial public realm of neighborhoods – architects, landscape architects, planners, traffic engineers, community developers, neighborhood associations, public officials; and especially developers. Anyone concerned with the lifestyle issues affecting the healthy development of today's children should read the compelling lessons of *Playborhood*."

— Robin Moore, Professor of Landscape Architecture, North Carolina State University

PLAYBORHOOD

TURN YOUR NEIGHBORHOOD INTO A PLACE FOR PLAY

MIKE LANZA

About the cover: This is a scene at the driveway of author Mike Lanza's house during Camp Yale, his neighborhood summer camp, in 2011. Kids are playing with legos on a mural map of his neighborhood during a session of Huntopoly. For more information on this driveway and Huntopoly, see Chapter 3, which starts on page 25.

Book design and production: The book cover and interior were designed by Michael Rutchik of Mudhaus Designs. Mike Lanza performed the layout and production.

For my sons
Marco, Nico, and Leo Lanza

CONTENTS

PLAYBORHOOD
MANIFESTO

I want my kids to
play outside with other neighborhood kids every day...

I want them to
create their own games and rules...

I want them to
play big, complex games with large groups of kids,
and simpler games one-on-one with a best friend...

I want them to
decide for themselves what to play, where, and with whom...

I want them to
settle their own disputes with their friends...

I want them to
create their own private clubs with secret rules...

I want them to
make lasting physical artifacts that show the world that
this is their place...

I want them to
laugh and run and think...

...every day.

That's what I had.
It's my standard for a good childhood.
It's my goal for my kids.

PART ONE

What's the Problem?

Identifying the challenges to free play today

A Social Problem

Back in 2004, when my wife was pregnant with our first son, Marco, I began to think deeply about his future in 21st-century America. The thought terrified me. I wasn't terrified that he would have an inferior education or live in an unsafe world. I was terrified that he wouldn't have a happy childhood.

Take a moment to think of the 10 best memories of your childhood before high school. Chances are, if you were born at least a few decades ago, most of these memories involve playing outside your house with friends, not scheduled events with adults around. To jog your memory, I'll offer my list from my childhood in the suburbs of Pittsburgh in the 1960s and '70s, not in any particular order:

1) Organizing and running a carnival with my friends for a muscular dystrophy charity in the Weisses' backyard

2) Playing stickball in the Bruces' backyard with the neighborhood guys every day one summer

3) Building a tree house in the woods behind the Allens' house and hanging out there with the guys

4) Wading with the Weiss brothers in hip boots down the stream at their farm

5) My first hit in Little League baseball, a triple to deep center, after a half-dozen games without swinging the bat at all

6) Seeing Pittsburgh Steelers' home games with my dad, especially Franco Harris' immaculate reception in 1972(!!!)

7) Golfing with my dad on Sunday mornings

8) Pickup softball and tag football in the street next to our house, especially all the weird rules we made up

9) Pickup hoops and H-O-R-S-E on the court behind the Morrisons' house
10) Kill-the-guy-with-the-ball games, especially the one when the guys conspired to dive and miss me on purpose, fooling me into thinking I had become the next O.J. Simpson

Hopefully, my memories have taken you back in time and helped you remember. Now that you have some great moments in mind, ask yourself, how many of those are possible for your kids today? For most American children, activities that involve play in neighborhoods with no adults around—seven out of these 10—are simply not possible.

You might say, "Of course, times have changed, but the American childhood of today isn't better or worse. It's just different."

Yes, it's different, but it's worse, too. A whole lot worse. Sure, we had television and organized sports back then. We just spent a lot less time at them than kids do today. Would I trade all my kill-the-guy-with-the-ball games for youth soccer? Not on your life. One thing we didn't have back then was a "playdate." How about building a tree house and hanging out there all summer vs. a dozen "playdates"? Are you kidding?

Because children are having a lot less fun and are dealing with heightened pressures and fears from parents, far more of them are experiencing serious emotional problems. The first sign, anxiety, appears, on average, at the tender age of 6. Behavior disorders start, on average, at 11, and mood disorders (primarily depression) start at 13. An incredible 22.2 percent of teens aged 13 to 18 suffer from mental disorders grave enough to result in "severe impairment and/or distress" (8.3 percent with anxiety disorders, 9.6 percent with behavior disorders, and 11.2 percent with mood disorders).[1]

The negative effects of the demise of neighborhood play go far beyond mere lack of fun or happiness. Because kids today spend so much time in front of screens, inhabiting virtual worlds rather than the real one, they lack strong real-world skills like face-to-face conversation or organizing a pickup ball game. Furthermore, because the majority of the time they spend away from virtual worlds is supervised by adults, they're "other-directed" far more than they are "inner-directed," to use the terminology of David Riesman in The Lonely Crowd.[2] In other words, they lack significant capacity to think for themselves. Robert Wuthnow, a sociologist, lamented, in referring to Princeton University students, "They are disconcertingly comfortable with authority. . . . They're eager to please, eager to jump through whatever hoops the faculty puts in front of them, eager to conform."[3] Thus, kids of today are far less healthy emotionally, and they have far fewer opportunities to develop social skills, leadership skills, problem-solving skills, independent thinking, and creativity. On top of all that, they're a heck of a lot fatter than we were.

But this isn't just about childhood. Free play, as it turns out, is a fundamental building block of a good life throughout the human life span, not just during the childhood years. That's because "activity oriented toward intrinsic goals, almost by definition, *is* play," according to research psychologist Peter Gray.[4] For many psychologists and psychiatrists, a life of intrinsic motivation is the most likely path toward a successful, happy life—a life in which one can have his cake and eat it too, so to speak. You may have heard of euphoric "flow" experiences—intense moments of intrinsic motivation applied toward a goal.[5] People who are intrinsically motivated do things because they want to, not because someone else expects them to. In general, they accomplish more than people who are motivated by external forces (like bosses and parents)—and they're healthier and happier, too. By playing freely, children discover intrinsic motivation and "acquire the skills and attitudes required for successful adulthood."[6]

Indeed, this lack of play in childhood is creating problems for teens and young adults. A wide-ranging study of children's emotional problems concludes, "Approximately one in every four to five youth in the U.S. meets criteria for a mental disorder with severe impairment across their lifetime."[7] More than 11 percent of young adults aged 18-24 in 2001–02 were found to have depressive disorders,[8] and almost all experts say these problems are increasing over time. A 2008 survey of university psychological counseling center directors reports that 95.7 percent of them believe that psychological problems have been increasing among university students in recent years.[9]

And what about intrinsic motivation? In *The Path to Purpose*, William Damon writes about a quality in teens and young adults (ages 12-22) that is directly related to intrinsic motivation: a sense of purpose in life. Nearly a quarter of his research subjects expressed absolutely no purpose in life at all.[10]

Depressing? I'd say so. Actually, I'm angry more than depressed. In general, we have more money than our parents did, but for some reason, collectively as a believe that parents who are truly fearful will be won over with these rational arguments. As will become clear later, I advocate an approach for solving the free play problem in this book that makes neighborhoods safer in perception and in reality.

The fundamental issue with problem frames 1 through 4 is that they imply individual solutions that directly amend the offending behavior (e.g., "Children are doing something too much, so if they do it less, the problem will go away."). However, the neighborhood play problem is more a social problem than an aggregation of individual problems.

For example, some parents in recent years have been trying to limit children's screen time and structured activities, and certainly I agree that parents should do this for their young children. However, using these strategies by themselves will generally not be successful in generating more neighborhood play because it frees up time for the kids who have limits, but it doesn't get other neighborhood kids outside playing.

Social problems are not solvable by simply telling people to change their individual behavior. Just as we can't solve a stock market crisis by telling investors, "Stop selling your stocks and start buying!" we can't solve the neighborhood play problem by telling our kids, "Unplug those electronics gadgets and go outside and play!" Many parents I know have done the latter, and, of course, their kids come running inside complaining that there's nothing to do outside, that it's "boring" out there.

In both cases, whether we're telling investors to "buy stocks!" or we're telling kids to "go outside and play!" it's extremely unlikely that large numbers of people would simultaneously take a leap of faith and heed the advice in lockstep, but that would have to happen in order for these proposed solutions to work.[15] Rather than trying to convince lots of people to change their individual behavior simultaneously, it's better solve a social problem through some sort of coordinated, social solution.

So, in *Playborhood*, although I acknowledge that there is some validity to these individual problem frames, I will emphasize a social framing for the free play problem. The single social factor that I believe, if changed, will lead to more children's free play is the attractiveness of their neighborhood. I'll frame the social problem *Playborhood* is aimed at solving as follows: "Neighborhoods rate very low in the minds of children when compared to all the other alternatives to allocate their attention and time." As a child would say, "Neighborhoods are B-O-R-I-N-G."

I should explain. A fierce competition for children's time and attention has emerged in the past few decades. Decades ago, free play in neighborhoods was practically the only option for children looking for something to do. Today, though, children have the Internet, lifelike video games, hundreds of television channels, dozens of new structured activities, and relentless marketing messages that draw them into malls and stores.

In the meantime, neighborhoods have gone backward. They're actually much less attractive to kids today than they were decades ago. They're still composed of streets and sidewalks and trees and lawns, but no children are out there. In essence, neighborhoods have been left in the dust. They're analogous to the 386 PC sitting in your garage, displaced by new powerful computers. Fortunately, as I'll show throughout this book, neighborhoods are far more "upgradeable" than 386 PCs.

CHAPTER 2

Children and Free Time

We know very little about how children make decisions for themselves. It's simply not a subject area that generates much attention or documented research from psychologists or behaviorists. In fact, the best research I've found on how children make decisions comes from marketing experts whose goal is to influence children to spend as much money as possible on their products.

The truth is that children are capable of making their own decisions from the time they start walking, but the scope of their decision making becomes broader as they get older. Parents control where their toddlers and preschoolers play and with whom, but they actually have little comprehension of the details of what their kids are doing. Although parents of elementary school-aged kids mandate that they go to school and attend certain structured activities, as well as dictating much of where they spend their free time, children at this stage gain some decision-making control over their playmates. In their tween years, children gain more power over the structured activities they participate in, and they also gain a fair amount of control over where they spend their free time. Finally, as teens, kids expend a great deal of their mental energy trying to figure out how to circumvent their parents' authority and do exactly what they themselves want to do.

An important theme of this book is that children should become self-reliant—able to function competently in the world on their own. So it is especially important for us to understand how they make decisions, and then to apply that knowledge to the particular problem of how they decide to allocate their free time.

The Allocation of Children's Free Time

It's obvious to anyone who pays attention to children's lives these days that they're not playing on their own very much. In fact, the most prominent researcher of how children's time is allocated doesn't bother to measure free play time. Sandra Hofferth's studies[1] have tracked the time children spend on "play" from 1981 to 2003, but, she admitted to me in an e-mail, "I expect free play would be a very small fraction of overall play." She also measures "sports," but she admits that this category is dominated by adult-supervised team sports.

That's absolutely striking. Pretty much anyone who grew up in the early or mid-20th century would tell you that all kids played outside on their own for at least an hour or two every day. I grew up in the late '60s and '70s, and my recollection is that all kids played outside almost every day when the weather was good, and when we did, it was for at least a couple hours at a time.

So, where have kids reallocated this enormous amount of time that they used to spend playing on their own, mostly outside? I describe the major categories of activities that have taken time away from outside play below.

School and Homework

According to the Hofferth studies, children ages 6 to 12 attended about six and a half hours of school per weekday in 2003, which is about one hour more than they did in 1981. They also spent roughly 45 minutes a day doing homework, vs. just under 30 minutes in 1981, for an increase of a little more than 15 minutes per weekday. So, in sum, children from ages 6 to 12 spent about one and a quarter hours more on school and homework per week in 2003 than they did in 1981. I suspect that this difference would be even greater if we had data from a longer period—from decades before 1981 and from a more recent year than 2003.

Structured Activities

"Overscheduled kids" and the parents who shuttle them from soccer to ballet to piano are prevalent in middle- and upper-middle-class neighborhoods. Although those children may learn to play an instrument or kick a goal, they are robbed of the chance to goof off, experiment, let their mind wander, and decide what *they* want to do before dinner, all crucial kid skills.

The Hofferth studies define two activity categories that could be grouped under "structured activities": "Sports" and "Art Activities," which includes not only visual arts, but also music, dance, and theater. Despite the buzz about the overscheduled child, the data in these two categories do not support the contention of many parents that the time children spend on structured activities has increased in recent decades. Between 1981 and 2003, the time that children have spent on these structured activities has remained fairly constant, at about 45 minutes a day.

Despite this overall statistic, it's clear that *some* kids are spending a lot more time in structured activities. Garey and Valerie Ramey find that, over the past few decades, all parents are spending more time with their children, but college-educated parents have increased that time by much more than the average.[2] They find that these college-educated parents focus their increased time on college preparatory activities—activities that are likely to help a child's college application a few years down the line. These include both extracurricular activities outside the home (team sports, arts, etc.) and homework. These are the children who are "overscheduled" in structured activities.

Screen Activities

Hofferth and John Sandberg's studies do not provide details on how much time children spend on electronic media. A Kaiser Family Foundation study done in 2009[3] shows that children between the ages of 8 and 18 spend seven hours a day consuming electronic media.[4] What's more, they're consuming almost 11 total hours per day of electronic media, but since they're multitasking so often, they cram this into seven hours of time. The researchers didn't even include one and a half hours of mobile phone talking and texting. So, if we assume the same rate of multitasking and add mobile phone time on to the seven hours of electronic media time, kids are consuming electronic media for about eight hours a day.

There is a significant racial difference in this statistic. African-Americans and Latinos average about two hours more than the average (10 hours a day), whereas whites and Asians average about two hours less (six hours a day).

Nonetheless, for all groups, this is a breathtaking statistic. Think about this. Sleep takes, say, eight hours. School takes about seven hours. That's 15 hours. Add eight hours of electronic media time and we're up to 23 hours. What else do these kids do besides sleep, go to school, and consume electronic media?

This addiction starts early. A majority of children less than a year old watch some television daily, and for them, the average is one hour per day. The percentage of children who watch some television daily increases to 90 percent by age 2, and children between 1 and 2 watch one and a half hours per day, on average, even though the American Association of Pediatrics advises *no* screen time before the age of 2, because of interference with crucial brain development.[5] Children between 2 and 5 consume television and peripherals (DVDs, game consoles) four and a half hours per day, and children between 6 and 11 consume four hours per day.[6] The drop is because non-TV screens—like computers and mobile phones—start to become important around age 6.

Although kids may be "consuming" these media at the same time that they're doing other things like eating meals, riding in cars, and doing homework, it's clear that they're also not playing outside. It looks as though electronic media have essentially squeezed outdoor play out of the lives of American children.

Playdates

"Playdates" are a common means for parents to exert control over who their kids play with, when, and where. Many kids have at least one playdate every day, but no formal statistics exist on how frequent or widespread they are. Although kids do make some decisions on what to play in these play sessions, they are a far cry from truly "free" play. The who-when-where restrictions end up constraining play quite a bit, and besides, a parent or other caregiver is always within earshot. Their presence diminishes the risks kids are willing to take, and some parents demand that kids stay inside so they can keep close tabs on what's happening. These factors make playdates very different from free play, and they greatly diminish their value.

How Children Decide What to Do with Their Free Time

OK, so we can agree that children have far less "free time" than they did decades ago because they spend much more time at school, doing homework, and in structured activities. Adults have a great deal of power over these non-free time decisions of children, especially when they are young, but this power dissipates as they get older. However, all children still have a great deal of free time (just look at all those hours spent in front of a screen!), and here, they are the primary decision makers of how they allocate it. In order to understand how they make these decisions, we need to get inside their heads, or at least do the best we can at this.

Imagine you're a 7-year-old kid today named Jamie (boy or girl? You choose. . .).

Inside your house, you have a half-dozen highly immersive PlayStation 3 video games with realistic 3-D images. You have a dozen DVDs of your favorite movies. Your television has hundreds of channels that you can surf for hours with a thumb on your remote.

Your school day is an hour longer than your parents' was, and on top of that, you have a half hour of homework per night, whereas they had no homework at your age when they were kids.

You're getting bombarded by marketing messages on all those screen media you consume and at school. Many of the products you hear about are sold at the local shopping mall, and some of your school friends have started hanging out there.

You dream of playing professional basketball and you've just joined a competitive team that practices three weekday afternoons and plays games every Saturday. Your parents insist that you take piano lessons weekly and that you practice at least a half hour a day.

In the meantime, your parents whine to you occasionally that you should play outside more. They tell you stories about how much fun they had in their old neighborhoods playing tag, building tree houses, and playing pickup sports games.

Unfortunately, you've never had any experience doing anything like what your parents describe. In fact, your neighborhood looks totally dead and boring pretty much all the time. It's just a mass of cars and trees and lawns: no kids or interesting activities.

So, how would you allocate your time? Would you make any effort to play outside in your neighborhood? Of course you wouldn't. Given all the forces competing for their attention today, it's no wonder that children are utterly uninterested.

Why Everyone Played Outside Decades Ago, and No One Does Now

Decades ago, most neighborhoods buzzed with kids playing outside daily. Today, hardly any neighborhoods have kids playing outside at all. This is perplexing. Is every kid in this generation really that radically different from kids decades ago? Of course not. What's more, many parents aren't that different, either. Some kids today aren't raised to be totally immersed in screen activities inside and structured activities outside. And there are lots of parents who played outside frequently as kids and think childhood should be about neighborhood play. Unfortunately, these facts don't make any impact on how many kids actually play outside.

Let's amend Jamie's hypothetical situation. Let's say that your parents have done a pretty good job of keeping you away from all these forces screaming for your attention and time. You're not hooked on any video game, and play one perhaps once a week. You don't regularly watch TV. You've chosen to focus on one structured activity, karate, which you attend one day a week for an hour and a half.

What's more, you love the idea of playing outside. You like all your parents' stories about their childhood exploits, and you enjoy watching reruns of the TV show *Leave It to Beaver*, in which kids get into lots of simple outdoor adventures.

So, you have this free play problem beat, right? You'll go outside to play often, right? Well, probably not. You see, your neighborhood's dead. The amount of free time you have and your affinity for neighborhood play don't change that. The neighbor kids have not escaped all the attractions of youth as well as you have, so they're never outside hanging out or playing. As a result, you don't play outside in your neighborhood in spite of the fact that you would like to. As a matter of fact, because you don't have the opportunity to play outside with other kids, you don't even consider it as an option when you have free time.

You're a victim of the "network effect," a phenomenon in economic theory in which the satisfaction that one person derives from consuming some "good" is dependent on how many other people consume that same good. In this case, the good is neighborhood play, which is one good in the "market" for kids' free time activities. The fundamental issue is that you will not be able to consume neighborhood play unless other kids do, too. Who wants to kick the can by himself?

Another example of a network effect good is a computer operating system. Many people avoid buying Apple Inc.'s Mac OS even though many industry experts claim that it is superior to Windows. Low market share for Mac OS means that it's difficult to find third-party software applications that work with it, making it less attractive. Thus, Mac OS's low market share creates a self-fulfilling prophecy, even though many experts think that it is superior.

The important lesson from the economic theory of the network effect is that it results in one of two outcomes: all or nothing. Network effect situations don't tolerate shades of gray. The network effect is not a two-party system; it's a monarchy. In economic terms, it results in a monopoly—i.e., a single, dominant solution. No outdoor play is the Microsoft Windows of childhood in America today. A large proportion of people wish it weren't dominant, but it is.

Why is this? Well, to return to Jamie, let's say there are two other kids on your block who think the same way about play, so Jamie's not alone, but he/she is still in the minority. For one reason or other, most other kids there are trapped in the dominant childhood lifestyle of screens inside or structured activities outside.

What's the probability that, on a given sunny afternoon, you will find something fun going on if you step outside to take a look? I'll call this the "probability of play" for shorthand. Intuitively, it seems that the probability of play isn't all (100 percent) or nothing (0 percent), but somewhere in between because there are other kids there who want to play outside. Instead, you might guess that the probability of play outside is, say, 20 percent.

Unfortunately, 20 percent is really bad—it might as well be zero. That's because your alternatives—a video game, a DVD, or TV—offer a 100 percent chance of success. In other words, if you try any of them, there is a 100 percent chance that you will be engaged at some level. What's more, they take less than a minute from the time you decide to try one of them to the time you start getting engaged.

On the other hand, neighborhood play has a much lower chance of success and takes a much longer time to investigate. So, you might try the neighborhood play option once or twice, but given your chance of success and your impatience, you're bound to fail and you're not going to keep trying it. You're going to give up and choose a sure thing. You'll develop this habit of ignoring the neighborhood play option, so that it drops off your list of possible things to do with your free time. The same thing will happen for the other play-minded kids on your block.

Thus, the probability of play for your block crashes down to zero, even though there are two other kids living on the block who would like to do it, too. Voilà—your block is dead as a doornail.

Decades ago, the outcome would have been different because your alternatives were far less attractive. Back then, if you walked outside to find something to do, you'd be far more patient, as were the other kids on the street. After all, if you turned around and went home, you didn't have any "sure thing" alternatives like a video game or 100-channel TV. And besides, your mom told you to get out from underfoot and come home at dinnertime. So, even if you didn't see any action when you first walked outside, you were much more likely to knock on a few doors. You might even have gone to the house of a kid who was not that excited about playing outside and tried to persuade him or her to join you.

Once you found a playmate or two, you would talk about what you're going to do. Because you had few if any attractive options at home, that conversation could have gone on for many minutes without someone bailing and going back home. Eventually, you all figured something out. You had fun.

The fact that you did all that hard work to find or develop something fun to do made it more likely that you and your playmates would go outside tomorrow and the day after. That's because you had laid the groundwork to make the fun more achievable the next time. Maybe you wanted to continue the game or project that you started, or maybe you wanted to try something different that you didn't have time for today. Either way, you had gotten a group together and some play started. Largely because of the lack of alternative things to do, you willed the probability of play to increase. Your neighborhood became a Playborhood, just like that. From today's vantage point, this may seem like an unlikely scenario, but it happened in countless neighborhoods decades ago.

This "all-or-nothing" quality of the network effect implies that neighborhoods today need a very big push to make the transformation from a zero-play neighborhood to a Playborhood. In other words, if you make a small change that makes neighborhood play a little more likely, you will probably still end up with practically zero play. To transform your neighborhood into a Playborhood, you need to attempt nothing less than fundamental culture change.

Marketers' Insights on Tweens' Decision Making

Up to this point, I've been utilizing what might be called a rational decision-making process for children, but that discussion ignores two important factors: 1) children's tastes—i.e., what they desire most; and 2) the emotional, irrational side of children's decision making. Consumer marketers have done a far better job than anyone else of understanding these.

In this section I'll highlight four insights on these factors from a particularly insightful book on marketing to tweens—children between 8 and 14—called *Brand Child*, by Martin Lindstrom.[7]

Peers' Opinions Matter More Than Parents'

Peers exert an extremely powerful influence over tweens' decision making. In fact, they displace the influence of parents, as tweens sometimes act as though they are going out of their way to contradict their parents' wishes. So, for example, most tweens will play video games and use social networking Web sites like Facebook, regardless of what their parents say, because so many other kids use them. In addition, most kids at this age will sign up for or drop structured activities largely according to what their friends do, not what their parents try to mandate.

If kids start to rebel against their parents in the tween years, the schism widens in the teen years. Clearly, as their tweens become much more social, parents must adjust their strategies for affecting their children's decisions. Otherwise, their relationship with their children may well end up dysfunctional and noncommunicative. I'll have more to say about the parenting transition from early childhood to the tween years in future chapters.

Lindstrom calls the most influential tweens "persuaders." These kids are the most popular. They are decision-making leaders, sometimes making new, risky choices because they know that other kids watch what they do and want to do the same things.

Obviously, it is much more important to win the participation of these kids in neighborhood activities than it is to win the participation of "followers." So, depending on the situation, you may want to offer some sort of enticement to draw persuaders' participation. At the very least, they deserve more attention.

Commitment to a Particular Decision Alternative Increases in Five Stages

Lindstrom offers a five-stage model for how a tween's commitment to a brand deepens as he or she becomes more familiar with it. For our purposes here, we can broaden this model to any decision alternative a tween might consider, not just which brand of athletic shoes to buy, but whether to, say, play outside and build a fort with some neighbor kids.

1) **Presence:** The child knows something about the alternative and about its attributes. Many children do not even know about what sorts of things they could do outside in their neighborhoods if they had an opportunity. Informing them of these things, either through stories from parents or through old

TV shows (like *Leave It to Beaver*) or movies (like *Stand by Me*), could help accomplish this goal.

2) Relevance: The alternative should "fit" the child's interests and values. A child who plays organized sports should know how he and neighborhood friends can play pickup games. Or, a child who is interested in art should be made aware of opportunities to create public art displays (from sidewalk drawings to a mural on a fence) right in his neighborhood.

3) Performance: At this level of commitment, children actually experience the alternative rather than just know about it. Performance is important because it makes a much more tangible impression on a child. So, for instance, the organized sports kid would play a pickup game with friends in the neighborhood, or the art kid would get to paint a portion of her house's fence.

4) Advantage: To reach this stage, an alternative should be able to claim some advantage, be it rational or emotional, over other alternatives. The organized sports kid would have to find something better about playing pickup games in his neighborhood than organized sports. Perhaps he likes playing anytime he wants without being on a schedule, or making up his own rules to add twists to the game. Or maybe he likes playing with his big sister, which is not possible in an organized league.

5) Bonding: At this stage, the child develops an emotional attachment to the alternative, so that he stops even considering the others. His identity may become inextricably linked to this alternative. Many tweens and teens these days are immersed in Facebook or video games so deeply that they lose track of the rest of their lives. Most of us would agree that "bonding" at this level of attachment can be unhealthy for children, but we must accept the fact that children do have a tendency to bond with certain free time activities. As a kid, I was so dedicated to playing stickball in the Bruces' backyard every day that I devised elaborate schemes to get out of our family summer vacation. (They didn't work!) How do we help our kids today to bond with a neighborhood play activity instead of with an indoor screen activity?

Bonding by Way of Ownership

In recent years, marketers have been experimenting with ideas for consumers to claim some ownership over the marketing messages for their products. For instance, dozens of organizations have run contests offering rewards to people who create the best video advertisements for their products or causes. Lindstrom cites the example of Jones Soda, which invited customers to send in photos of themselves for possible use on a Jones Soda label. They got 60,000 entries for 40 possible labels per year.

Promotions like these have been very successful at getting consumers to think deeply about these products and causes. In effect, the consumers who submit entries become de facto salespeople.

In the context of neighborhood play, I believe that children should be afforded much more ownership of the physical configuration and look of their neighborhoods than they are commonly given today. Driving down most residential streets, it's very uncommon to see any personal touches created by children like forts or artwork. Some parents may argue that these artifacts are best left in backyards, but in that case, far fewer people get to see what the kids have done, so far fewer people are impacted by their children's statements of ownership. These parents don't want their yards to look to others like they were decorated by their children, but that is in part why their children aren't bonded to their yards as play spaces.

Chapter 12 describes how you can create a neighborhood hangout that your kids can personalize.

Tweens Only Consider Leaders

Because they are so conscious of what their peers think of them, tweens are completely uninterested in brands that aren't leaders. Lindstrom writes that tweens "simply do not buy brands that do not lead in their field."[8]

Neighborhood play is generally ignored by tweens when they think of fun things to do. No tween wants to play outside unless it looks *really* fun to his or her peers. This point supports the conclusion of the previous section, namely, that small, incremental steps to get kids outside playing may ultimately have no effect at all, and that only big and bold steps have a chance of succeeding. Neighborhood play needs to be really, really cool. If tweens change their minds about it only slightly and think it's just OK rather than totally B-O-R-I-N-G, they'll probably still ignore it as an alternative.

In Part Three, I'll describe the steps you can take to create the most vibrant neighborhood possible for your kids. But first, let's take a look at what some innovative neighborhoods across the country are doing.

PART TWO

How Are Neighborhoods Solving This Problem?

Profiles of neighborhoods that are making free play a priority

CHAPTER 3

Yale Road: Menlo Park, Calif.
An Oasis of Play in an Affluent Suburb

All I have to do is look hard enough, I thought, and I'll find a house we like for sale on a block where lots of kids play. Then, I'll buy the house and we'll move there. Problem solved.

I went out one nice Saturday afternoon and drove down block after block after block in the towns in which we wanted to buy, Palo Alto and Menlo Park, Calif. I passed by a lot of finely manicured lawns and parks with adults hovering over kids on playground equipment, and I even found a kid here or there without an adult, walking somewhere or chatting with another kid. However, I didn't find anyplace where kids were playing on their own with abandon, like my friends and I did in my childhood neighborhood. So, I went out searching again the next Saturday. Then I went out one or two times more, until I had driven slowly through practically every street in those two towns, some streets many times, before I gave up. No luck. Zilch.

I had three choices: 1) buy our favorite house and forget about my quest for a childhood of neighborhood play for my kids; 2) look outside of Palo Alto and Menlo Park; or 3) buy a house in a promising neighborhood and work to transform it into a Playborhood. Most people would have chosen the first option, but I had no intention of waving the white flag. The second option didn't seem like a solution at all, the more I talked to other parents and realized that kids weren't playing much anywhere. So, I opted for the third option.

To paraphrase Robert Frost, taking that third option has made all the difference.

It's taken a heck of a lot of time and financial investment, but our neighborhood is a pretty decent Playborhood now. We still haven't reached the standard of my childhood neighborhood, but my kids play outside rigorously for at least an hour each day, and they're thriving because of this. Best of all, we're all enjoying our lives here immensely.

In this chapter, I'll describe the steps we've taken to make our neighborhood into a Playborhood, and the results of all those efforts.

Privilege Without Play

Palo Alto and Menlo Park are places of great privilege. Their next-door neighbor is Stanford University, one of the richest and most prestigious universities in the world and the birthplace of Silicon Valley giants Cisco, Google, and Yahoo. Harvard may have been the birthplace of Facebook, but the founder, Mark Zuckerberg, relocated that company to Palo Alto early in its history. He just moved the company to Menlo Park. Menlo Park's Sand Hill Road is the home of the worldwide venture capital industry. The median price of a home in Palo Alto in 2010 was $1.6 million. One of Palo Alto's two high schools, Henry Gunn High School, ranked No. 67 in the nation in 2011, according to *U.S. News & World Report*.[1]

On the other hand, Gunn High is also the home of a teenage suicide epidemic. In 2009, in the space of six months, four students from that school took their own lives by walking in front of a speeding train at the same train crossing, all at different times. At some point, the Palo Alto Police Department stationed a patrolman at that crossing 24-7, and it claims to have prevented eight to 10 other possible suicide attempts there.

Clearly, something is very, very wrong with childhood in Palo Alto and Menlo Park. How could children who have so much be so unhappy?

Well, I would argue that they don't actually "have so much." Their childhoods are far more stressful than they are happy. As I described earlier, they hardly play outside at all. Instead, they're inside in front of screens or doing homework, or they're outside of their neighborhood at some adult-run organized activity. Many kids here, perhaps a majority, are very highly scheduled. The extreme pressure for children to achieve so they can get admitted to a selective college filters all the way down to preschool. Play is definitely not a cultural priority around here.

Neighborhood Play Evangelism

Why do union members picket the businesses they are striking against outside the entrance? Why do political protesters gather and march together in public places?

Why do I prefer that my kids and I play in the front of our house rather than in the back?

We all do these things at least in part because we're trying to make an impression on passers-by, and ultimately persuade them to join us. Unions and protesters have learned over the years that this strategy works. The more often they put bodies out in public, and the more bodies they have out there, the more outsiders will take notice of their cause.

And so it is with play and neighborhoods, I've found. If you don't care if your kids play more with other neighbor kids, by all means, have them to play inside your house or in your backyard. However, if you want your kids to play more often with neighbor kids, you need your kids to be out front at every opportunity.

My kids are out in our front yard quite often, for some time every day when the weather is good. When this pattern began when Marco was 4, I was out there with them pretty much all the time, but at this point, they're on their own at least half the time. They ride bikes, rollerblades, or scooters; they play bouncy ball games, basketball, and street hockey; they play in the sandbox or build forts. There's absolutely no planning involved. In other words, this is no "playdate" culture.

Three factors serve to pull them to our front yard often. First, "screen time" is not an option for them—they hardly ever watch TV, play video games, or interact with computers (see Chapter 13). Second, our yard is full of very fun features, which I'll describe shortly. Finally, I take them out there often when I'm not working—on weeknights when it's light outside and weekend days.

Because of this, we make our play visible to neighbors on a regular basis, and this draws other kids over. We reach out to get them to join us as well. We knock on doors often. The first two times I took my two older boys to knock on the door of one neighbor family with kids of similar ages, they didn't answer the door, even though I was sure they were home. The mom explained to me later that they never imagined that someone other than a stranger would knock on their door unannounced. Now they, as well as many other neighbors, regularly knock on our door and others'. My wife and I frequently send our oldest son Marco out to knock on a neighbor's door by himself to seek out a playmate.

I've let it be known that neighbor children are invited to play here anytime, whether we're here or not, and many children do come by, some with their parents and some without. Since my boys have few structured activities, they're usually here when those neighbor children come by. During the nice weather months, which last from April through October here in Northern California, we have at least one big spontaneous gathering of neighborhood kids every week.

We also host planned events at our house at which all neighbors are welcome. During the spring and summer, we have a big kid event in our yard about once a month. Two of my sons have summer birthdays, which we always celebrate in our yard, but we also find many other excuses to hold events here. These are, almost without exception, the best kids' parties I've ever attended in terms of the amount of fun kids have. Kids yell and laugh and run nonstop until their parents drag them away kicking and screaming. All kids who play here, mine included, reach a level of sheer joy that I hardly ever witness in kids outside of our yard.

In addition, we make a special effort to publicly celebrate two kid holidays every year: Easter and Halloween. We co-host an Easter egg hunt with neighbors, and we welcome hundreds of trick-or-treaters to our front and backyards every Halloween with outdoor music, special effects machines (a bubble maker, a fog machine, and a black light), and all the wonderful play features of our yard.

There's no question: We've made huge efforts to make our neighborhood's atmosphere more friendly, and we've clearly made a difference in that regard. In the final section of this chapter, I'll assess what we've accomplished and what I'd like to improve.

Our Yard as Neighborhood Hangout

I've completely renovated our front and backyards to make them into kid hangouts. My wife and I want our kids to spend most of their waking hours outside our house rather than inside, weather permitting. So, inside our house, we only have one screen for our kids to use, and it shows no live TV or computer content. It has an AppleTV attached to it, and we use it to listen to music, see photos, and watch an occasional YouTube video or DVD.

We've also spent almost zero money or time decorating inside our home, and it shows. All our furniture is well-worn. One leg broke on our fake leather couch recently, so I took all the legs off and we could continue to use it. Now, it's at a toddler's level. We call our decorating style "Early Childhood." Our focus is outside our house because we want our children to be focused out there.

I don't think we'll get a new couch at adult height until Leo, our youngest, hits his adolescent growth spurt.

On the other hand, I've invested a great deal of money in our yard. Some of the features I've installed, particularly our backyard features, are out of financial reach for many families. However, scaled-down versions of most of these features can be just as fun for kids.

I hope readers of this book will re-evaluate the relative budgets for the inside and outside of their homes. When the weather is OK, a great yard is far more important to kids than the inside of their house. Moreover, even in bad weather months, kids don't appreciate expensive decor at all—and besides, I've never met a kid who doesn't like mucking around in rain boots or snow gear. Having a great home entertainment system or a home theater inside the house is attractive to them, but they'll benefit far more from a great yard. It may seem strange to forego living room furniture or an extra bathroom or a home theater to invest in your yard, but if you can begin to think that way, your kids will have happier, more fulfilled lives.

Besides money, I've invested a great deal of time into planning our yard space. I've scrutinized every square inch with an eye toward how we could best use it. Practically all front yards have features like walkways and driveways to move people and cars in and out, but architects and builders hardly ever think about kids actually passing time there. They are often dominated by beautiful plants, not play features and seating. Backyards are often better equipped for children to use, but they also have a lot of unused space.

Here are some features of our front and backyards, many of which are easy to implement in a variety of locales.

Front Yard

Whiteboard: We put outdoor-capable whiteboard material[2] on the existing fence that runs along one of our borders. The entire stretch of whiteboard runs more than 30 feet. We also keep a wooden box there with dozens of dry-erase pens.

Picnic table with storage benches: Our sturdy 8-foot picnic table lies under a redwood tree about 10 feet from the sidewalk. The picnic benches all have weatherproof storage, meaning that the top surfaces are hinged and can be opened to store things inside. We store things there like disposable plates and cups, books, and board games.

We love having meals at this table during warm months, both family meals and dinner parties with guests. You might think it's strange to have meals so close to the sidewalk and the street, but it's a bit like eating at a sidewalk restaurant on a city street. Actually, it's better, because we always see neighbors we like passing by, and sometimes, one or two sit down to chat with us. Neighbor kids often join our kids when they leave the table to play in the front yard or the street. I've come to enjoy dining in our front yard so much that I now consider eating in our totally fenced-in backyard claustrophobic and lonely.

Here's a wide view of my front yard about a year and a half before I published this book. Since taking this photo, we've added some new features such as our driveway mural.

To the left is our picnic table with kids sitting on the storage benches. To the right is one panel of the whiteboard, which has a projected image on the far right. This was projected from inside the storage bench in front.

Media system: We also store a media system inside one of the picnic benches. This consists of an AppleTV, projector, audio amplifier, and speaker. The projector shines through a piece of plexiglass installed at one end of a bench and is aimed at the whiteboard. I control the AppleTV using Apple's Wi-Fi-enabled Remote application on my iPhone, so I don't have to open this bench to operate it. Most frequently, I use Remote to play music on the AppleTV and the AppleTV projects photos on to the whiteboard via its screen saver. My kids love this, and it adds to the fun of hanging out and eating outside. I sometimes play fun YouTube videos there when one of my kids requests one. These days, they've been requesting videos of parkour or free running—forms of urban acrobatics in which participants run and jump and flip on and between buildings—so they combine video watching with their own experiments in acrobatics. On festive occasions I play videos. For instance, on Halloween, I've played *The Wizard of Oz* or *It's the Great Pumpkin, Charlie Brown*.

Showing photos and videos in our front yard does not bring a couch potato lifestyle out there. We have no couches in front of our whiteboard, and besides, with all the other fun things we have to do in our front yard, no kid sits watching for very long. It just adds to the "cool factor" there, making it more of a magnet for kids.

Fountain: The most prominent spot in our front yard, bordered by the sidewalk and our driveway, is occupied by a fountain. I chose a fountain design that children could play with safely. It has no standing water, no sharp edges, and a very low profile—about 16 inches off the ground. It's extremely popular with toddlers and dogs passing our house, so it acts as a "gateway" to invite families into the rest of our yard.

Concrete driveway with mural: We tore out our driveway's "pavers" stones with somewhat convex surfaces laid in a pattern—and laid smooth concrete in its place. Everyone said I was crazy because they thought our pavers were much prettier than concrete. But I didn't do this for aesthetic reasons. Who cares how pretty your driveway is, anyway? Instead, I was concerned with our kids being able to do things like scooter, skateboard, rollerblade, ride bikes, play basketball, and draw with sidewalk chalk. Our kids do all that and more on our driveway now, every day. Activity there is enhanced by a neighborhood mural that we installed there. The map shows a few blocks in our neighborhood with our house in the center. Lot lines are drawn in and addresses are written so kids can find their house. They can also add a Lego house on any lot because the lots accommodate a 32 x 64 peg Lego base plate. Streets are also "HO-scale," so Hot Wheels cars and HO trains fit in there.

Here's Nico playing with a towel in our fountain at the age of 2. That summer, he drenched his clothes playing there at least twice a day, every day.

Our driveway has a colorful neighborhood map mural.

As it turns out, no feature of our front yard gets more use than our smooth concrete driveway with the mural. Needless to say, we keep our cars parked on the street.

Neighborhood mosaics: Kids at Camp Yale, a neighborhood summer camp I run every year, have helped make two mosaics that are installed on the fence next to our driveway. Both were designed and built by a friend of mine who's a mosaic artist, but kids' contributions play an important role. The designs are both inspired by children's books that are special for my family: *The Big Orange Splot*[4] by Daniel Pinkwater and *Roxaboxen*[5] by Alice McLerran.

The first mosaic has houses that look like the ones on our street, plus a wonderful quote from *The Big Orange Splot*: "Our street is us and we are it. Our street is where we like to be and it looks like all our dreams." The latter is a depiction of a *Roxaboxen*-inspired village that we've built by a nearby creek (see the next section for more on how we use our creek). Roxaboxen is the true story of some kids in a Yuma, Ariz., neighborhood who built a play town out of rocks and found objects. That mosaic has the quote "And so it went. The seasons changed, and the years went by. Roxaboxen was always there."

It's absolutely wonderful to have beautiful artwork that's so meaningful to our children embedded into our front yard.

Play river: Our fountain entices toddlers, but older kids want to do a lot more with water than just splash their hands in it. They love sending both manufactured

3.6 MOSAIC This is the mosaic inspired by the book "The Big Orange Splot."

boats and handmade boats, usually made of corks and sticks, down our play river. They also move rocks around in the water to change currents for boat races. Our river was created by Riveropolis (riveropolis.com).

Basketball hoop: These are a very common feature of many families' driveways, but they're usually not very well used. Ours gets more play because of the number of kids who stop by our house. Once they're here, older kids in particular always shoot a few hoops.

Sandbox: This is another big draw for toddlers. I've placed it right next to our driveway and about 12 feet from the sidewalk, so it's prominent. I often come home to see a toddler playing there with a parent or nanny hanging out close by.

To up the appeal, I purchased kilos of relatively worthless foreign coins at eBay, and I've given them to my boys to bury in the sandbox, as well as in the backyard. Other kids are always thrilled to find coins, and they get really excited when we let them take their booty home.

Backyard

My wife and I debated a lot about whether to install lots of play features in our backyard because, being surrounded by high privacy fences on all sides, it's not easily accessible to neighbors. Thus, this would seem to violate our objective of creating an inclusive neighborhood hangout. We decided to go ahead and install the best features we could back there for three reasons:

Some kids won't stop playing with our play river until their parents tear them away.

1) Our city prohibits us from installing many play features in our front yard because it does not allow "permanent structures" there. The playhouse and play structure that are in our backyard would be classified this way. Also, our backyard's in-ground trampoline would be difficult or impossible to install in our front yard because it requires an excavation, and this would be difficult to get approved.

2) We have more space for play features in our backyard than our front yard. To ignore it would be a waste of space.

3) We hoped that we could entice other neighbor kids to come into our backyard even if it's more difficult to access than our front yard. For one thing, we've told all neighbor kids that they can venture into our backyard on their own, whenever they want. Many have taken us up on this invitation, entering our backyard from the front driveway along a path next to our house. In addition, we've tried to get our neighbors who share our fence on three sides to agree to open gates between our yards. We haven't succeeded at that yet, but kids from two adjoining yards hop the fence and come over often thanks to a ladder we've set up for that purpose. Due to all these efforts, about once a week, we get unannounced visitors in our backyard. We like that a lot!

Here is a list of our backyard play features:

In-ground trampoline: There is no stronger "kid magnet" than our in-ground trampoline. It's our single most popular yard feature by far. If you want neighborhood kids to flock to your yard, this is the most effective solution. Any kid old enough to jump well—around age 3 and up—absolutely loves jumping on a trampoline. The problem with typical aboveground trampolines, however, is that they are very dangerous for children. In-ground (i.e. ground-level) trampolines like ours are safer than aboveground trampolines that are surrounded by nets, according to the American Academy of Orthopaedic Surgeons.[3] Elevated trampolines with safety nets are more dangerous for two reasons: 1) they are surrounded by padded steel poles that hold the net up; and 2) when the nets get old and tear, as they always do, the danger of falling all the way to the ground increases. We have yet to have a serious accident on our trampoline after three years of very frequent use with few restrictions.

But besides the safety aspect, an in-ground trampoline is a great deal more fun for kids and adults because it's so easy to access. No one has to haul it out or grant permission for it to be bounce time. Kids can casually start jumping on it after they've been running around doing something else. It's also a lot more fun for those who aren't jumping because they can sit around it and socialize. In our backyard, we have outdoor beanbag couches totally surrounding two sides of our trampoline, so this area can accommodate a very large social gathering.

Play flows between the grass and the in-ground trampoline very seamlessly.

If you can find space for a trampoline, the only problem is the cost. To install an in-ground trampoline, you need to get someone to dig a big hole and build a retaining wall around the edges of it. The cost of doing this is likely to be much more than the cost of a quality trampoline. As for the latter, I purchased one specifically designed for in-ground use from webounce.com for about $1,700.

Playhouse: Our faux log cabin playhouse has two stories and lots of extras. I purchased it from Home Place Structures (homeplacestructures.com), a company that sells many models of playhouses and will customize practically anything. The house I chose is much larger than the basic model in every dimension, with a complete second floor and slides in the front and back. We received the components of the house in a flat shipping pallet, and a carpenter assembled the house and slides and added many other features.

Inside, we added whiteboard walls on the first floor and painted drywall on the second. Kids love writing messages on the whiteboard, which I expected. What I didn't expect was that they would also write graffiti all over the painted drywall of the second floor. When I first saw this, I was bummed, but I quickly came to realize that children had found a unique outlet to express themselves and a way to claim ownership over their new space. This was their place, free from the rules of the regular house—and isn't that what a playhouse should be?

On the second floor, we keep mattresses that fold up so we can shove them aside when we're not using them for sleeping. When we open them up, we can cover the entire area and sleep five to six people. In a few years, I'm sure my boys will have the most sought-after sleepover venue in the neighborhood.

Outside, my carpenter added a porch swing, speakers, LED lights, rock climbing toeholds, and a skylight on the roof. The speakers, connected to an Apple Airport Express inside, stream music from a computer inside our house. I control this anywhere with my iPhone and Remote software. The kids get *very* energized to jump on the trampoline when they hear their favorites tunes, which, not coincidentally, I like a lot too: James Brown, Kool and the Gang, the B-52s, and the Talking Heads! The rock climbing toeholds are also enormously popular. Practically every kid 5 or above, plus many adults, have used these to climb to the apex of the roof.

Swing set: Our swing set is very sturdy due to its heavy-duty steel A-frame design, and has places for three different swings. We swap in and out four differ-

We decorated our playhouse as a haunted house for Halloween a few years ago.

ent swings there: a conventional swing, a glider, a baby swing, and a horizontal tire swing.

Nature Hangout: The Creek

We're very fortunate to live two and a half blocks from a creek that offers ample opportunity for natural exploring. Since we moved here three years ago, I've helped my boys and neighbor kids develop a real attachment to it.

In winter and spring, when it has running water, we build dams to cross it or wade up and down it. When it's cold, we wear wet suits, and when it's warmer, we wade in with sandals and shorts. In summer and fall, when it's dry, we hike along the creek bed, build forts, and collect things like rocks and golf balls. (A golf course

Marco wades into the creek in his wet suit.

is a mile or two upstream.) We pass a lot of time at the various forts they've created there, especially the play village patterned after the one in *Roxaboxen*. We also take a metal detector down there on occasion and dig up old metal scraps. With these we become amateur archaeologists, positing theories on how things ended up there. When I'm not leading an archaeology expedition, I usually park myself at a nice rock and let the kids wander the creek bed on their own. They always find a way to occupy themselves at every moment, and are reluctant to leave.

I hope that when my boys and their friends get a bit older, they'll go to the creek frequently on their own, without an adult accompanying them. They're headed in this direction. It often seems when we're down there and I'm sitting on a rock that they forget that I'm there at all. If my hope is realized, the creek and its environs would fulfill two vital roles for them. It would be their place to explore nature on a regular basis on their own, and it would be a neighborhood hangout totally owned by them, unlike our yard.

We usually don't encounter another soul the entire time we're down there, which is surprising considering how wonderful it is and how many people live so close to it. It's amazing to me how little the children around here know about the area right where they live. Instead, most of their parents drive them all over the place every day. They experience nature when they get driven to some faraway park once every week or every month. It would be so much easier for them to just walk five or 10 minutes down to our creek.

Overcoming Obstacles to Free Play

Notwithstanding all the work we've done and the tremendous progress we've made in increasing play activity in our neighborhood, our house is not the daily social headquarters for all kids around here. Although all neighborhood kids have been here at least a few times, a number of them don't return that often.

One reason for this is that Marco isn't nearly as welcoming to all neighbors as I am. He's quite shy. My wife and I repeatedly ask him if he wants to play with certain other neighborhood kids, and he often declines. Moreover, he's often not very kind to these kids when they come over. Sometimes, he'll get into a selfish spat with one of them. Other times, he'll simply walk away from the other kid to do something else.

My wife and I have worked hard with Marco to diminish these antisocial tendencies. Specifically, we started out by scheduling a lot of one-on-one play between Marco and other kids in our yard, and monitoring these at arm's length. We're not fans of playdates in general, but we considered these to be a "stepping-stone" for Marco to work on his social skills. In the beginning, our yard was a bigger draw for kids than Marco was, but now, Marco's become a much better friend to his buddies. Although he's still not as welcoming to other kids as we'd like him to be, problems rarely occur anymore, so we no longer monitor his play sessions. If your child has the same challenges, I encourage you to keep working at it rather than avoiding having neighbors over.

If you find, as we have, that your efforts don't always generate immediate change in your neighborhood, don't be discouraged. Remember, unanimous, enthusiastic approval from all neighbors is not likely. No matter what you provide in your own yard, and how enthusiastically you extend invitations, not everyone is going to take you up on the offer of neighborhood play.

I've noticed that when I make a very visible push against the status quo of our peaceful neighborhood, we stick out. After all, I'm aiming to change a culture. It'd be a heck of a lot easier to just stay inside until we need to drive our kids to school or soccer practice. I'm trying to do the very hard work of making our neighborhood a much better place to play, so I step outside of my comfort zone a bit and take a chance that I'll ruffle some feathers.

In our neighborhood, I've encountered a whole range of reactions. On one end of the spectrum, many enthusiastic families come by to say "hi" frequently and play. One of these families from a few blocks away brings their kids to our yard practically every day. On the other end of the spectrum, I've encountered a small amount of direct opposition. One father originally opposed our front yard renovations because he thought they would lower his property values. I amended our plans a bit, and now he and his kids are among our closest friends in the neighborhood. (By the way, it's pretty clear to me that if we've impacted his property value at all, we've increased it.)

My kids and I had a wonderful day recently collecting fall leaves from up and down our street into one huge pile until the neighbor whose house this pile was in front of threatened to "file an action" against me. My first impulse was to yell back and tell the guy to "make my day," but instead, I bit my tongue and move the pile a few feet down the street. I felt bad for my boys that this neighbor damaged what had been a wonderful experience of working together, and I felt that I would only add to the damage by getting into an argument with the neighbor. Moving the pile together turned out to just add to our fun.

In another case, a mother asked me to stop helping Marco (age 5 at the time) climb over our back fence to play with her son, even though the boys always had a great time playing together. She felt the fence hopping was invading her privacy. I accepted her wishes and no longer let Marco climb over the fence unannounced, but I was sorry that our sons were deprived of this spontaneous opportunity to play. Fortunately, the boys continue to ask for one another, and occasionally skirt around this "unannounced visit" rule.

Most neighbors lie somewhere in between these two examples, with most being approving and visiting our yard on occasion. However, there are a few neighbors who are unenthusiastic about what we're doing here.

My approach has been to stay the course as long as the positive responses outnumber the negative ones. When I do get a specific negative reaction, I try to accommodate whatever complaint the neighbor might have. I take this approach because, on the one hand, I know that the environment we're creating really is appealing to kids, but on the other hand, I know that open feuds are terribly corrosive.

Through it all, my boys and I just keep playing outside, having fun. That creates an irresistible attraction for parents, but even more for kids as they grow up and become more able to make their own decisions. Marco has asked me more than once at the end of a really fun day, "Can we live here forever?" I take that as the ultimate vote of confidence.

The Choice to Lead Alone

Neighborhood politics are particularly risky for me because of my determination to steer our neighborhood toward cultural change on my own, without working closely with any other neighbors. Thus, I have no political "cover" if someone decides to try to obstruct my efforts.

Most of the other Playborhoods described in this book have a vital advantage over mine on Yale Road in that they have very solid community buy-in. Residents there feel a sense of ownership in their neighborhood, and this ensures higher participation rates, as well as a richer culture. In addition, widespread participation by neighbors increases the land area that can be devoted to a neighborhood hangout and the financial resources behind it.

So, why didn't I take community-based approaches like those other Playborhoods? I started taking some pretty aggressive steps to change the culture of our neighborhood less than a year after moving in. At that point, coordinated action just wasn't possible. One might argue that I should have waited a few years so that I could work toward a community effort among my neighbors, but I wasn't willing to wait that long. Plus, I suspected that I could succeed in building a vibrant community with fairly broad consensus much more quickly by acting boldly first on my own.

So far, this strategy has been working quite well. Just three years after moving in here, our neighborhood is clearly much more vibrant. In addition, my family's relations with all close neighbors is quite good. So, I can see that we're on the way to creating a great Playborhood in a very short time.

The State of Play

I'm happy, but not entirely satisfied, with the neighborhood play lives of my kids. My wife is, too. She's an enthusiastic supporter of what I'm doing here, but she lets me take the lead on it, for the most part. I really appreciate her patience—I've done some pretty radical things here, and made a few waves, but she believes in the importance of free play as much as I do.

We're happy because, practically every day, they're outside playing and having fun. They're pretty independent for their ages. At 7 and 4, Marco and Nico frequently play outside for extended periods of time with no adults watching them, and Leo (2) is out there on his own for short periods playing as well. Lots of neighbor kids come over to our yard to play, almost every day, weather permitting. Some feel perfectly comfortable coming over uninvited, and many even bring their playdate friends over to our yard.

Plus, we have those amazing kid parties here. Both at these parties and at countless other spontaneous events, kids have total unbridled joy here. It's a very, very good life for my boys, my wife, and me, as well as for our neighbors.

So, how can we do better?

Fundamentally, I want to see more kids outside more frequently, playing together. Still too often, no one is outside playing during times when children are not in school. My boys are outside more than most kids in our neighborhood because my wife and I are so committed to this. It would be a lot more fun for them to be outside if other neighbor kids were out there more.

If more kids were outside at one time, they could play complex games that small groups of kids just can't play. These complex games—pickup sports games like softball, football, ultimate frisbee, and street hockey, plus chase games like capture the flag and hide-and-seek—force children to develop strong leadership, social, and moral reasoning skills.

My kids, particularly Marco, could be doing more to get other neighbor kids outside. Although I don't need for him to be an aggressive play promoter like me, his shyness and social challenges often get in the way of his pursuit of what he wants—kids to come out to play with him, and friendships with those kids. Of course, getting lots of kids to come over to our house should, in theory, help him overcome these problems. I do see that it's working, but solving these problems is a long, gradual process.

Finally, I'd like to see my kids and neighbor kids create multiday projects as part of their play. Yes, they've built a Roxaboxen village in the creek by our house, but that was largely orchestrated by me. I look forward to these kids, on their own, building forts and huge arts and crafts projects and secret societies that take lots of planning, resources, and time. These kids are still a bit young for this sort of play—the oldest kid who plays at our yard frequently is 9—but it's great for learning, and it's also very fun.

Huntopoly: A Neighborhood Bonding Game

My neighbor, Karen, is a widow with grown kids, and my family probably never would have gotten to know her if not for our great Huntopoly encounter last summer.

Huntopoly is an innovative new game I invented at Camp Yale, my neighborhood summer camp. It's a mixture of a scavenger hunt and monopoly, and the goal is for campers to get a lot more comfortable with particular places and people of our neighborhood . . . and for our neighbors to get to know us, too.

My idea for Huntopoly started with my driveway map mural, which I also designed. It's colorful art on our driveway that also serves as a platform for children's neighborhood play.

To begin, teams choose a monopoly piece and block on the driveway. Unlike in Monopoly, each piece stays on its respective block all week, never crossing paths with another piece. To start each day's game activity, each team rolls the dice once and moves its piece that number of lots on the dice. Each team then ventures out

Karen is smiling widely with, from left, my sons Nico and Marco, and a friend.

A boy reaches to move his giant monopoly piece down Princeton Road. Above his piece is a Lego house he and his teammate created from a previous turn.

into the neighborhood with an adult or teen facilitator to find the house on the lot its piece is sitting on. When the team arrives there, the facilitator first takes a photo of the team in front of the property, and then the team walks up to the front door and rings the doorbell.

If no one is home, team members run back to the Huntopoly board in my driveway and roll the dice again to move their piece and get a new house assignment. If someone is home, team members try to get a list of items, shown below:

1) photo of team w/ resident
2) first and last name of each resident (including pets)
3) an interesting fact about the resident(s) that they'd like neighbors to know
4) 1 cup cocoa powder
5) small object from resident for driveway map
6) photo of team's favorite thing in yard or house
7) flower from the yard
8) rock from the yard

Note that the ingredient that each team obtains for item 4 above is different. We pull all the different ingredients together to make a cake for our Huntopoly party on Friday. Before leaving a house, team members give the resident an invitation to invite him or her to the Huntopoly party on Friday morning. The team gets points for every resident (including pets!) that come to the party.

When they get back to the Huntopoly board, they must put all items they collected on the lot on the driveway map, and they can also optionally build a Lego house on that lot to get more points.

Of course, you don't need a beautiful Huntopoly board on your driveway to organize a neighborhood scavenger hunt. You can implement many of our ideas, such as a neighbor name hunt, a neighbor photo hunt, or a race to collect ingredients for a cake. The point is to figure out fun ways to get kids out in your neighborhood learning its geography, features, and above all, its people.

Lyman Place: The Bronx, N.Y.
A Safe Refuge for Play in a Poor Urban Neighborhood

One of the poorest neighborhoods in the United States, the South Bronx, N.Y., is home to a remarkable play street. It didn't happen overnight. Back in the 1970s, life in the South Bronx was so bleak that arsonists, hoping to recover insurance money, burned more than 40 percent of all housing there. Today, arson is no longer a major problem, but the poverty remains severe for residents, primarily African-Americans and Hispanics. New York's 16th Congressional District there is the poorest district in the United States, with 49 percent of children there living below the poverty line.[1] How has this place become home to a vibrant Playborhood?

When Hetty Fox moved back into her South Bronx childhood home at Lyman Place in 1970 after a few years teaching college in Southern California, she was aghast. "There were very few people, and there was a lot of deterioration, many empty apartments," she said. "People had a sense of general despair."[2]

In the decades since then, Fox has made a concerted effort to make Lyman Place a safe, inviting place for both kids and adults by playing both "neighborhood defense" and "neighborhood offense."

Neighborhood Defense: Keep Long-Term Residents

To Fox, the first key to turning Lyman Place around was keeping long-term residents there who have connections to each other. This is what she calls "neighborhood defense." "A new resident may see things and not know how to interpret them," said Fox, explaining her rationale. "So they shy away from saying anything, whereas an older resident might speak up right away, 'What are you doing here? You know, you have no business here!' They take an initiative."[3]

Her first action was to advocate on behalf of longtime residents of a city-owned building on Lyman who were being forced to move away. The city wanted to consolidate residents into fewer buildings to save money on maintenance, but it was oblivious to how this would affect neighborhoods. "They were the ones who looked out the window, and that is a plus!" said Fox of the residents who were about to be displaced. "At a time when there was so much marauding and vandalism going on, we needed people who were interested enough to keep an eye open for the safety of the block."

Fox's advocacy persuaded the city to keep that building operating and let those residents stay there. Shortly thereafter, she and other neighbors started the Lyman Place Improvement Committee, and the city housing office told the committee it could "invite," or refer, particular people to get into city housing on Lyman Place. The invitation of the committee got a great many people into this housing. Most of those they invited were former residents who had moved away before, or relatives of current residents. For example, they invited Catherine Pierce, a woman who eventually raised a total of 13 children (some her children, others her grandchildren) on Lyman. Pierce moved back shortly after two of her daughters, and shortly before two of her sons.

Today, the extended family of Catherine Pierce is very prominent on Lyman Place. Lynnell Wiggins (13), a great-grandchild of Catherine Pierce and current resident there, looked outside Fox's second floor window one recent June evening. "There's a cousin of mine there, a friend there, and oh—there's another cousin," she said. "Some blocks you can't go out, even 7 a.m., without getting shot or something. Everyone who can comes over here, everyone who doesn't want trouble. [Other than here] I mostly don't go anywhere."

Fox agrees that the presence of familiar people makes children feel safer at Lyman Place. "Kids here feel a comfort, they feel like this is home. They feel like if they're outside playing, they're safer. They feel like there are people who are watching, and those people are aware, because they're at their windows. . . . The children feel protected because there are people who have already shown an interest in who these children are and will tell their mother if they're doing the wrong thing. . . . This way, they know they're being corrected with love, not 'I'll call the cops on you.'"

While neighborhood defense keeps out the bad influences, neighborhood offense is about making children's lives better—making them happier, healthier, and smarter.

Neighborhood Offense: Create Healthy Options for Kids

Shortly after her first victory saving the building on Lyman Place for long-term residents, Fox started her first major effort for kids: an after-school educational center. Having graduated from college and worked as a college instructor in black studies, Fox acts as an educational role model for children there. She teaches kids about diverse topics like the geopolitics of world energy and how to count to 10 in the many languages she's found spoken in the surrounding South Bronx neighborhoods, including Russian, Zulu, French, Arabic, Japanese, and Hebrew.

From the seeds of the educational center grew the idea of a summer play street, free of cars, that would allow kids to interact outside. For most neighborhood children, a lack of safety and parental supervision meant long days in front of the TV

Hetty Fox (right) gazes down the street on a lazy summer day on her play street. Photo: Ozier Muhammad/The New York Times/Redux

Fox created this flyer's artwork by hand to publicize the 2010 play street.

and no sense of community. Fox discovered that for the city to designate Lyman Place as an official play street, she had to gather signatures from at least 51 percent of residents expressing their support. Going door to door, she spread the word about the benefits of play for families here. After tireless effort, she got her 51 percent, and has done so year after year, for 35 years running. One longtime resident summed up the consensus view back in 1984, "Simply put, she is our savior."[4]

The children of Lyman Place are its best advertisement. They freely share how the play street makes them happy and improves their outlook on life. "As far as being able to have fun somewhere in the summer, this is it, so we cherish it," said Reginald Taylor, 17. "It's good to be around positive people."[5] Rahmel George, 16, says simply, "All the kids are happy. I'm happy."[6]

Still, it's important to note that the play street does have some vocal opposition. For example, one man across the street from Fox runs a junk business out of his garage, so not being able to drive a truck up to the garage during summer days is a big problem for him. Others don't have children and find not being able to park on the street during the day inconvenient. But so far, the value of the play street has triumphed, operating every year since 1977.

Fox starts preparations for the play street every morning at 8 a.m. by banishing all parked cars and setting up barricades at both ends of the street. Then, with assistance from a few paid youth workers, she sets up the regular play equipment like a basketball hoop, a volleyball net, jump ropes, a nok hockey table, and Mancala, a West African board game. They also set up tables and chairs and, on occasion, arts and crafts materials like sidewalk chalk and paints.

Kids of all ages bring their scooters and skateboards. During my visit, I noticed one toddler, Jacob, just 2 years old, enjoying the play street without any direct adult supervision—something rarely seen on a typical American street. Fox explains, "His cousin Andrew is right there, and everyone else here knows him, too. Besides, he has lots of aunts and uncles and cousins who live right here on the street, as well as his grandmother and grandfather. In fact, his great-grandmother lives here, too." Everyone knows Jacob, and looks out for him—giving him the opportunity to explore in a way that many parents can't imagine for a child of his age.

Indeed, one of the prime benefits of the play street is that children have a unique opportunity to play freely, enabling them to explore their own identities in a safe place. Kids from toddler age to teens find friends and community there. "This program helps the children. It lets them play, be who they are, develop their own character," said Genashia Robinson, 17, a play street youth worker.[7]

In the late afternoon hours, as parents return home from work, Lyman Place becomes a very large communal family room. Kids play and parents socialize out-of-doors and get to know each other. It's a magical time, when it's easy to forget that it's in the midst of one of the most dangerous, bleak places in America.

Rahmel George, a frequent participant of the play street, says, "Miss Fox is a very good leader to me. She's a good woman for doing this for 34 years. If I ever get some money, I'm gonna bring it right back to the play street because I got big dreams."[8]

5

Share-It Square: Portland, Ore.
An Intersection Where Kids and Adults Play

It's fun to just sit at a corner of Share-It Square at the intersection of SE Sherrett St. and SE 9th Ave. in Portland, Ore., for an hour or so on a nice day. On a map, it appears merely as one of Portland's thousands of four-way intersections, but it's a very unique place. Any time of day, you're likely to see pedestrians hanging out there talking, laughing, playing with their kids. However, for sheer humor, it's even better to watch the occasional passing driver who's never seen this intersection before.

Upon seeing the colorful mandala painted on the pavement, the unique features on each of the corners, and the people who often crowd around them, uninitiated drivers will invariably slow down to a crawl and gawk. Their reaction is like that of rubberneckers who lose all their concentration on the freeway when they see a couple of cars crunched up on the shoulder. It's difficult to say whether they're upset, pleased, or just completely dumbfounded.

Share-It Square resides in the currently trendy Sellwood neighborhood in Southeast Portland, but before the Square was built, it looked like a fairly ordinary middle-class place. In fact, it had crime problems that made it much worse than ordinary. One year in the 1970s, a U.S. Marine was beaten to death and a 57-year-old grandmother was raped and killed.

Young architect Mark Lakeman moved into a house his father owned close to what is now Share-It Square in 1987. Frustrated with what he saw as his profession's lack of concern for human relationships, Lakeman came to the conclusion that the American model of development is flawed because it results in fragmented, unsustainable communities. So, he embarked on a multiyear international journey to learn about how vibrant communities outside the United States are built and how

Share-It Square is easily one of the most interesting-looking city intersections you'll ever see. In the foreground is the mandala from 2009, and in the background is the Kids' Klubhouse.

they function. He spent time in the villages of such diverse places as Tuscany, Italy; Oxford, England; and the rain forests of Central America.

Shortly after returning to that same house in 1996, Lakeman began putting his new insights on common space to work in his neighborhood. One of his fundamental realizations from that trip was that people needed public gathering spaces right where they live, yet most city planning codes prohibit the building needed to create these spaces. He describes why making streets into rich community resources is important:

> In America, our great archetype is the main street, which is not really a center. It's just a flow. It's a movement corridor, and you have to yell across the street because there isn't a place in the middle. There isn't a social commons that you can attain and occupy. Putting the public space back where it's supposed to be may not sound like a huge change, but it has a profound effect on the social culture. Everybody needs it even though they don't know it's missing.[1]

He also learned a fundamental lesson from a Lacandon Maya elder: "Never ask permission to build a structure that brings people together. Just build it."[2] Keeping that lesson in mind, he decided to build a small, open structure of recycled materials situated between large trees at the front yard of a property on the corner of the intersection. Lakeman knew very well that it violated the Portland building code,

The casual, funky T-Hows, erected at what later became Share-It Square, was the birthplace of the City Repair movement.

but he went forward with his experiment anyway. "It was built to make a point," Lakeman said. "It was a catalyst to raise an issue, to make people aware of the necessity of place and informal social rituals."

The "T-Hows," as he called it, was a place for neighbors to eat, grab a cup of tea, and chat. It was wildly popular. First a few, then dozens of people came by every week. It was a magical summer of social discovery and awakening. "So, by the time the city said, 'You can't do that!' there were all these people who were like, 'Oh, yeah? We're going to do something else.'"

Indeed, Lakeman and his neighbors started doing something else even more public and permanent. They created a plan for transforming the intersection into a public square, which eventually became Share-It Square as it exists today. They began building features for each of the corners, like seating and message boards, but the centerpiece was the colorful design that they planned to paint on the pavement of the intersection to mark this special place.

In order to paint, they would need a city permit to block off the streets. Lakeman and his neighbors made a pitch to Portland's Transportation Department, but they were rejected. However, on their way out of the building, they were pulled aside by a department official who was sympathetic to their cause. "Where I come from in Brooklyn, we used to play in the street. It's the only community space we had," he said. He quietly granted them a permit for a block party and told them to do what they felt they needed to do.

On the day of the permit, they had a big painting party on the street, completing the entire design. Once city officials heard about what they had done, they threatened big fines for vandalism, so they appealed to the City Council and to the mayor of Portland, Vera Katz. Although they were certainly breaking laws, Katz was impressed that they were also creating community, slowing traffic, and reducing crime, all at no cost to the government. She set in motion what finally became official city recognition and support for "Intersection Repair" in Portland, and the City Repair (cityrepair.org) organization was born with Lakeman as founder. Since then, City Repair has helped residents transform dozens of other spaces across Portland, both intersections and other kinds of spaces, into community gathering places.

These intersections are unique Playborhoods in that hundreds of drivers and pedestrians who don't live in the immediate vicinity pass by them every day. Their very public nature makes them self-promoting; with nonresidents passing by, it's more likely that the idea will spread to other neighborhoods. Although Lakeman would welcome it if the streets forming the Square were closed off to car traffic, he likes the fact that "a driver doesn't have to park his car and walk a block to interact with this place. I want him to see it. So, people being able to just flow right through is really powerful." He adds, "When a driver comes to a sudden stop, parks, and gets out of their car to check the place out . . . that's inspiring." The fact that these are public intersections, and not people's private yards, also invites participation by all who pass by; you don't have to live here to play here.

A cornerstone of City Repair's mission is to help residents to create community-oriented places right where they live. The organization believes that localization—of culture, of economy, of decision making—is a necessary foundation of community sustainability. It has grown to be a viable nonprofit organization in Portland with a handful of employees and dozens of dedicated volunteers.

Mark Lakeman at the book exchange stand. Anyone can take a book anytime, with the informal rule is that you replace it with a different one in exchange.

What Draws Neighbors to Share-It Square?

Share-It Square is recognizable by the colorful design painted in the center of the intersection. Lakeman and his neighbors paint a new one there every spring during "Village Building Convergence" (VBC) a 10-day event coordinated by City Repair in which neighbors throughout Portland build new community-oriented features or renovate existing ones. There is also at least one structural feature on each corner designed to promote socializing or sharing. These are hosted by the residents who live on those corners, but clearly, they are all collaborative efforts that are widely accepted by the community. The Kids' Klubhouse is a funky open-air structure cobbled together from a living tree, dead branches, and recycled building materials—a kind of fort, complete with seating and toys. Other structures include a book exchange station for sharing used books, a chalk message board, a community bulletin board, a custom couch sheltered by a grass-covered pergola, and a solar-powered tea station.

In addition to hanging out in this space, though, another aspect of the community building is the time and energy residents spend maintaining the square—tidying up, making repairs, or replenishing the tea station. Share-It Square gets lots of use, so litter gets left there, items end up out of place, and features get broken. Neighbors bond and feel a renewed sense of ownership by working together and taking pride in the space.

Besides routine maintenance, Square-area residents meet periodically to discuss changes or enhancements to the square that they will perform at VBC. In addition to painting, Share-It Square neighbors participated in two other projects at the 2009 event: the "Cat Palace" and the "Living Roof Installation." The days of the VBC are like a festival for the neighborhood, particularly the day when the intersection is closed off to traffic so it can be painted. On that evening, everyone feasts at a potluck party.

Residents also get together frequently in other times of the year for purely social events. Some of the social events take place at the Square, such as the spectacular wedding of Mark Lakeman and City Repair co-founder Lydia Doleman in 2007. Area residents also have numerous get-togethers throughout the year that have nothing to do with the Square—because after all, they all know each other well now.

The Impact on Kids' Lives

Although Lakeman and most of the other original Share-It Square pioneers back in 1996 were single adults without children, families have become very prominent in the community in recent years. Families alter their walking route to swing by the Square to see who's there. Community participation—by both adults and children—in upkeep or additions to Share-It Square create a foundation for the fluid social relationships of families there. Resident Adriana Ferbel-Azcarate notes that her son feels an intense sense of ownership for the painting of the mandala. When

Two boys play in the Kids' Klubhouse one afternoon. For the most part, all the toys stay there, unstolen and undamaged, day after day,

he learned from his mom that car traffic causes it to wear out over the year, he told his mom, "We should keep cars from driving here!"

She also noted, "When I first moved here [to the United States] from Mexico 13 years ago, I met hardly any neighbors." Despite the fact that hardly any Latinos live near the Square, she developed deep connections to neighbors for the first time since she immigrated. When she and her husband had an opportunity to buy a house, she resolved, "I'm not living anywhere else. There's no way."

One of her best friends there is Miriam Habafy, a native of Morocco who is equally enthusiastic about living in the area. "I love it here," she said as we watched her boys bounce on a nearby trampoline—set up in a neighbor's front yard as a shared play space—in the twilight. "I can't imagine raising my boys in another neighborhood."

CHAPTER 6

The Waters: Pike Road, Ala.
A New Urbanism Community with a Focus on Family

I had a hamster when I was a kid. I thought he was really stupid because I controlled his behavior merely by placing him in a cage with a wheel. He would run and run and run on that wheel forever. Didn't he realize that he wasn't getting anywhere?

I was reminded of that hamster when I first heard the claims of New Urbanist architects about how their designs can make inhabitants of their developments more sociable with each other, more neighborly—an idea criticized by many with the term "physical determinism." I thought, "Humans are not hamsters! We are intelligent beings with complete free will. Our behavior and our underlying motivations can't be controlled by an architect!"

Certainly, I accepted the idea that architects could design "easy-to-use" buildings that would enable us to do what we want to do more efficiently, like get ready for work in the morning in our bedroom+closet+bathroom. However, the claims of the New Urbanists went much further. They seemed to say that their designs could somehow get us to do things we didn't even consider doing before. For instance, a couch potato in a nondescript suburban tract with no public space would become a chatty neighbor at a New Urbanist development.

Still, even if I was suspect, I was also intrigued by this claim. After all, it fits with my deep desire to give kids vibrant neighborhoods with abundant play opportunities.

I went searching for a New Urbanist development that was explicitly aimed at encouraging kids' play, and I found The Waters in Pike Road, Ala., whose Web site featured a video called "Kids' Paradise." I was still skeptical. I knew very well that marketers are very good at creating false images. Besides, parents like the ones interviewed in this video often view their own neighborhoods through rose-colored glasses. After all, in my housing search in California, I had encountered countless parents who said their neighborhoods were great for kids, but when I visited many of these, I rarely saw even one kid outside, having fun.

So, I decided to jump on a plane and see The Waters for myself in early 2008. I visited the first "hamlet," Lucas Point, which was the only one built at the time.[1] My verdict from that trip: We're hamsters. The Waters *is* a children's paradise. It's a wonderful place for adults, too.

How Does New Urbanism Influence Play?

New Urbanism is a movement in architecture and urban planning aimed at reviving community life. The "new" part of the name is a bit ironic because New Urbanists aim to re-create the charm of classic old urban neighborhoods that fell into decay after World War II, when nearly all development resources came to be dedicated to sprawling suburbs.

The enemy of New Urbanists is the automobile-based lifestyle of suburbs. Most suburban tracts have lots of homes and few, if any, attractive destinations within a walkable distance. Thus, streets come to be dominated by automobiles. The design of these tracts supports a lifestyle of staying inside the home or of driving out to other destinations, so there's not a lot of outside play happening in these places.

New Urbanism's design features are aimed at drawing people to venture outside their homes on foot, and to encounter each other. Public space is emphasized and privacy is de-emphasized. The idea is that, by seeing each other often, people will tend to develop trust for one another and get along well. "Sharing the same public realm, these [residents] have the opportunity to interact, and thus come to realize that they have little reason to fear each other."[2] Suddenly, neighbors who would normally zoom past each other on their way to other places become friends—and their kids have opportunity to play with one another on a regular basis.

Of course, communities that are alive with pedestrians rather than cars are usually good for children. Children thrive both because there are other children outside to play with and because they can wander freely with little fear of being hit by a car or abducted by a stranger.

This aerial view of Lucas Point was taken before all buildings were built, but nonetheless, it shows a very self-sufficient community. The treed areas in front are common parkland, and the large building just past that is Town Square, the retail center.

The Waters has implemented all the major community-friendly features of the first New Urbanism development in Seaside, Fla., designed in the 1980s by the pioneering husband-and-wife architect team of Andres Duany and Elizabeth Plater-Zyberk. These are worth keeping top-of-mind no matter what community you're looking into:

- **Walkability:** Each hamlet is designed so residents can walk to any other point in less than 10 minutes, giving it a small-town feel.
- **Low or no fences:** There are few fences, and those that exist are very short, offering a feeling of openness and making it easy to see people in their yards.
- **Small yards:** Houses are very close to the street, so front yards are small or nonexistent. Side and backyards are small as well. This encourages people to leave their properties and spend time in the many common spaces (see below).
- **Lots of common space:** Surrounding the homes are numerous common spaces such as courtyards, broad medians, and open fields. These are very accessible and well used by residents. In one field, builders dumped a great deal of dirt to create a hill that has been dubbed "Playborhood Hill."

- **Narrow streets:** Cars can't speed through the streets because they are very narrow and people are often walking on them. As in many old European cities, pedestrians rule.

- **Integrated retail center:** Retail shops, a few offices, and a restaurant/bar are concentrated in an area called "Town Square," a community hangout. Residents commonly walk there, rather than drive.

- **Integrated recreation facilities:** The Waters boasts tennis courts, lakes with plentiful fish, common lakeshore land including a sandy beach, a play structure, and a swimming pool, all within easy walking distance to residences.

- **No cul-de-sacs:** Cul-de-sacs are often considered desirable in suburban neighborhoods because they represent a refuge from dangerous traffic. However, at The Waters, all streets offer such refuge, so cul-de-sacs would only serve to socially isolate those who live at the end of them.

- **Big front porches:** All houses have big front porches, and some also have second floor balconies overlooking the street.

The restaurant at Town Square is the most popular social hangout for residents of The Waters. Chance encounters with friends are virtually unavoidable. Note that the toddler at the lower left is running across the street with no adult around.

Naturally, since the New Urbanist model markets itself as a family community with plenty of shared spaces to play, it creates a self-fulfilling prophecy to some extent. These developments attract lots of parents who want more outdoor play for their children, and, voilà!, kids who move there find other kids outside to play with. In addition, many of the developers actually live on-site, making them more invested in the community and more apt to spearhead changes and improvements.

The layout of The Waters also encourages a level of spontaneity that can seem impossible to achieve in a car culture. Resident Amy Neuenschwander says, "There's no need for planning ahead because we live within walking distance of each other. So, you hang out at the pool on a Saturday, and at about 4 o'clock, everybody starts getting hungry and we decide whose house to go to. All families just come together, and 'bring what you have.' It's very easy to enjoy each other's company when it's that low stress. The kids entertain each other and the parents all get to have parent night, too."

Kids slide down "Playborhood Hill," a couple of large mounds created by dirt from an excavation. It's quite common to see groups of kids at The Waters playing without an adult in sight, as is shown here.

Where Can One Find New Urbanist Communities?

Although New Urbanist principles have strong influence over architecture and planning throughout the United States, full-fledged New Urbanist communities (also called TNDs, for Traditional Neighborhood Developments) are still concentrated in the Southeast portion of the United States, and there aren't many of them. Below is a list of the best TNDs for families, compiled by Nathan Norris of PlaceMakers, who worked on the founding team at The Waters and has lived there since its inception.

Northeast

- The Kentlands in Gaithersburg, Md. (by Washington, D.C.)

Southeast

- Baldwin Park, Orlando, Fla.
- Celebration near Orlando, Fla. (famously developed by Disney)
- Habersham, Beaufort, S.C.
- I'On in Mt. Pleasant, S.C. (near Charleston)
- Mt. Laurel, outside Birmingham, Ala.
- Norton Commons, Louisville, Ky.
- River Ranch, Lafayette, La.
- Serenbe, outside Atlanta
- Village of Providence, Huntsville, Ala.
- The Waters, Pike Road, Ala.

Midwest

- Middleton Hills, Madison, Wis.
- New Town, St. Charles, Mo.

Mountain West

- Daybreak, South Jordan, Utah
- Prospect, Longmont, Colo.

Pacific

- Hercules Waterfront, Hercules, Calif.

The Playscape Revolution: Iowa City, Iowa

A Natural "Playscape" in Every Yard

Tony Malkusak, a landscape architect in Iowa City, is on a mission. He's working on a model to create a fun, vibrant "playscape"—a nature-based landscape made for play—in every yard in America.

He's already taken the first crucial step: He's created a prototype playscape in his own backyard for his four youngest children. He treats his yard like his laboratory. "We landscape architects and contractors spend so much time focusing on what we build, but what really matters is how it affects families' lives for years after we're gone," he says. "Over the last five years, I've gone through, oh, 30 or 40 iterations here. I'm still out there trying new things practically every weekend."

Nonetheless, it's not too early to call his yard an unqualified success. "Our yard is *the* hangout for our subdivision. It's the hub," he says. "Depending on the time of year, I'll often see at least a half-dozen kids out there, and many of these kids aren't mine. I've seen as many as 12, 13, 14 kids out there on many occasions."

Many Iterations of Design & Build

The first thing he did was dump a truckload of play sand in his backyard. Later, he built a pergola to serve as a gathering place, and built two large sandpits and filled them with the play sand. Then there was the stone stairway; the swing with high back for his son, Anthony, who has hypotonia (low muscle tone); the deck; the chalkboard and storage shelves; the bench; the swing set; the tunnel; the water rapids

Multiple groups of kids engage in different activities simultaneously in Malkusak's backyard.

and pondless waterfall; the prairie, a half-acre area with wild grasses that don't need cutting; the vegetable garden; the berry patches; and a stage for kids' performances.

The kids have a great deal of control over the evolution of their yard. For one thing, when he's not installing features on weekends, Malkusak watches how kids use the yard. From those observations he gets his many ideas for new features and adjustments.

He also created a "Secret Sandtrap Society" for kids to come up with ideas more explicitly. For instance, the society has requested that Malkusak replace a small circulating fountain with a more elaborate water feature, a pondless waterfall and rapids. "When resources become available, I will build it," he said dutifully.

Kids also have a great deal of control over what their backyard looks like day to day. "There isn't the pressure of, 'Oh we've got to be pristine and cleaned up every time you leave the site,'" said Malkusak, who enjoys seeing kids' works in progress. "This shows the kids that we value what they're doing."

The most outstanding example of this lies in the 3,000 pounds of "river jacks"—3- to 6-inch round, flat, smooth rocks—that he acquired a few years ago. He stashed them somewhere because he couldn't use them for the purpose he had intended, but kids ended up taking them all over the yard to make things like army guy forts, sculptures, houses, and a mud kitchen.

By being so close to the kid culture that formed around their playscape over five years, Malkusak has gained many unique, fundamental insights. Other landscape architects design one iteration and leave, never living through the cycles of trial and error that he has.

Creating a Playscape Model for All Families

Now, he's working on a project to leverage these insights for five new playscapes in the Iowa City area. Like his own, the playscapes for this project will emphasize children's social play and nature. Their cost will be roughly the same as a typical backyard landscaping project with a boxed play structure, according to Malkusak.

"We're trying to put a car in every garage," he said, alluding to Herbert Hoover's 1928 presidential campaign slogan. "In an average backyard in the Midwest, if a family's installing some playground equipment, a typical landscape, and turf grass, the total cost is anywhere between $3,500 and $12,000. That's a typical transformation, so that's the price point that we're shooting for."

Malkusak's organization, Abundant Playscapes (abundantplayscapes.com), is partnering on this project with Nature Explore (natureexplore.org), which is an outgrowth of the Arbor Day Foundation. Nature Explore is a well-established organization that has built numerous playscapes at public venues like schools and parks, but this is the organization's first project in residential playscapes.

These two organizations, along with another partner organization, Backyard Abundance (backyardabundance.org), have chosen five families to participate in the program. First, the partner organizations run a design session with each of the families to create a design for each yard. They have the family fill out a 25-item questionnaire, and they walk through the yard with family members to get their thoughts on their present yard and their wishes for a renovation.

Standing at the entry gate to Malkusak's backyard playscape are Nancy Rosenow, executive director of Nature Explore, John Rosenow, executive director of the Arbor Day Foundation, and Malkusak. The plaque on the right announces this yard's official certification as a Nature Explore Environment, the first such honor for a residential yard.

Nature Explore records the results of this meeting as the "before baseline" for its qualitative study on these projects. The next day, Malkusak creates a proposed design that the organizations and the family discuss in a meeting that night.

As of now, all five of these meetings have been completed and the designs have been finalized.

Now, the organizations and the families are preparing to implement the new designs. The next step is for Malkusak to give the family a bill of materials to purchase from a local home supply store. Then, the family buys these materials and brings them home.

On "build day," the family members and some neighbors meet with Malkusak to implement the new design. He plans to provide as much guidance as is necessary, but needs will vary widely. "A couple of dads among the five families have construction experience, but on the other end of the spectrum is a doctor who doesn't know

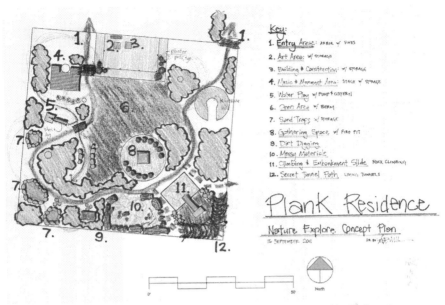

Key:
1. Entry Area: ARBOR W/ VINES
2. Art Area: W/ STORAGE
3. Building & Construction: W/ STORAGE
4. Music & Movement Area: STAGE W/ STORAGE
5. Water Play W/ PUMP & CISTERN
6. Open Area W/ BERM
7. Sand Traps W/ STORAGE
8. Gathering Space, W/ FIRE PIT
9. Dirt Digging
10. Messy Materials
11. Climbing & Embankment Slide. ROCK CLIMBING
12. Secret Tunnel Path. LIVING TUNNELS

Plank Residence

Nature Explore Concept Plan

16 SEPTEMBER 2011

North

This is the design drawing for one of the family playscapes designed by Malkusak.

which end of a hammer to hold." Still, the participation breeds a sense of ownership and camaraderie among the neighbors who will ultimately share the playscape.

Finally, Nature Explore will interview family members, and possibly neighbors as well, and complete a before-and-after qualitative study report on these projects. Malkusak and others will take the results of this report and reflect on their own experience to fine-tune their design-and-build process.

"Most families aren't going to go through what I've done to re-create my backyard as a play space, but I want them all to have what we have," he said. "My kids are outside with neighbor kids practically every day, running around creating their own stuff. Imagine if we could duplicate that end result thousands of times over!"

"Well, I think we can. . ."

N Street: Davis, Calif.
A Retrofit Cohousing Community

Do you remember sleepovers with friends or going to sleepaway summer camps? Did you ever live in a college dormitory, a fraternity or sorority, or other shared housing? Wasn't it fun? Many adults count the communal living experiences of their youth among the fondest memories of their lives.

So, what happens after we grow up? Why do we all choose to live totally separate lives in separate houses?

Most of you have probably never asked yourself that question seriously. Instead, when you become an adult, you do what the rest of society does—join adult society and accept separate lives as a fact. One person who never bought into this part of "adult society" is Kevin Wolf. After graduating from the University of California at Davis in the early 1980s, he continued living in a communal house in Davis, where he and his colleagues shared meals and housekeeping responsibilities. They tended an organic garden in the backyard and enjoyed the vegetables for their meals. Wolf bought that house in 1984, and his partner, Linda Cloud, bought the adjoining house a short time later. They tore down the fence between those houses to expand the garden, and held common dinners across the two houses. Even though they hadn't read about "cohousing" (introduced to the United States in 1988 through husband-and-wife architectural team Kathryn McCamant and Charles Durrett), the tearing down of fences between those two houses marked the real beginning of the N Street cohousing community.

The idea proved to be infectious. Soon, other neighbors tore their fences down and regular neighbor dinners got larger and larger. Today, N Street is a bona fide cohousing community with about 20 households and about 60 people sharing one

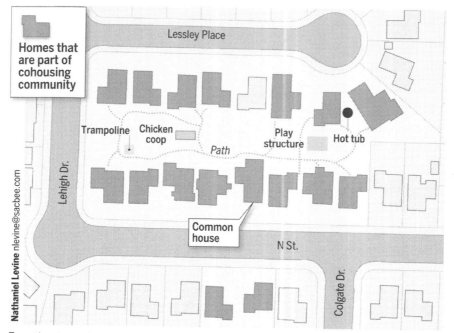

Lessley Place

**Homes that
are part of
cohousing
community**

Lehigh Dr.

Trampoline   Chicken
              coop   Path   Play   Hot tub
                                    structure

Common
house

N St.

Colgate Dr.

Nathaniel Levine nlevine@sacbee.com

From the street, the houses look like all other houses in that part of Davis. The interesting area is the common backyard—the lack of fences, the shared facilities, and the vibrant community spirit one can almost always find there.

common, fenceless backyard. In the early 1990s, members led by Wolf and Cloud turned one of the houses there into a dedicated "common house" for shared dinners, parties, and other entertainment like foosball and television watching. N Street has become a very vibrant community with a distinct, homegrown culture. The many children who have grown up there play a very important part in that culture.

Other than its origins, N Street is typical of the hundreds of cohousing communities in North America. One significant characteristic of all these communities is that residents manage the neighborhood through a nonhierarchical community process. At N Street, community members make joint decisions on things like furniture in the common house, how common dinners are run, the staging of special events, aspects of the backyard, and media relations for the community. In addition, they closely regulate new entrants into the community.

Neighbors as Extended Family

Everybody I spoke with at N Street referred to fellow community members like family. Wolf and Cloud's daughter, Kelsey Wolf-Cloud, grew up at N Street and now lives abroad. "When I go back home, it's the people in the community that I hang out with, not my outside friends," she says. "Friends on the outside come and go, but my friends at N Street are family."

One of the most important foundations of this are the dinners that take place at the common house three or four times a week. Each of these dinners is prepared by a small group of residents. The feeling of the common house is like a college dormitory's dining hall. People share large tables and talk, and afterward, some linger to play foosball or watch television.

Residents' everyday lives are woven together in countless other ways. Adults run into each other in the common backyard or on the way to other shared facilities like the laundry room or the compost pile. Kids can't help but play with each other because their backyards, devoid of fences, all merge into one. They all share the trampoline, the open field, the play structure, and the paths and trails.

An unspoken rule at the Wolf-Cloud house is that a visitor should walk in without knocking. Wolf-Cloud says, "We prefer that people just come in. Knocking bothers the dog." Even on nights when there isn't a community dinner, several people of various ages from different households typically gather for dinner at the Wolf-Cloud house.

On the night I visited, a 15-month-old Chinese girl named Lucy was part of the group. At first, it was difficult for me to figure out who Lucy's mother was. Besides the fact that all the adults there were Caucasian, I watched three different adults help her throughout the evening. A middle-aged man put her in her high chair and a woman put food on her plate. Another woman, named Rebecca Hammann, fed her. Later, I learned she had recently adopted Lucy. As with the meal and the dinner banter that followed, everything felt shared quite equally between the guests.

After visiting N Street that day, I came away thinking that we're all fools for living with fences between us, for eating alone every night, and for not dropping in on each other on a moment's notice. At that one routine dinner I experienced more neighborly warmth and camaraderie than most people experience in a year.

Age 4 in this photo, Lucy is thriving as a member of the N Street community.

The Impact on Kids' Lives

"People always ask me if it was difficult being an only child," said Wolf-Cloud, "but I always thought I had about 10 other siblings."

Jacob Taylor, who also grew up there, said, "There was almost always someone around to do something with if you felt like it. And, it was perfectly OK to knock on doors and see if anyone was home and say, 'Hey! I'm bored. Are you?'"

The whole N Street community gets involved in raising children there starting from a very young age. As a result, preschoolers feel very comfortable wandering about the community.

One adult who gets very involved in children's lives there is Pamela Walker, who moved to N Street a few years ago and quickly became one of the community's most active members. Recently, she took some initiative to make an innovative play space in her front yard for preschoolers.

"I was noticing that the kids we have here now are younger, and we really don't have a set-aside area that the young kids could relate to," she said. Walker's solution was to create a zoo for the plastic animals that were laying around all over the community, a "Plastic Fantastic Zoo," in her front yard. "We have exhibits of dinosaurs, dragons, rain forest critters, spiders, space aliens, wrecked cars, game pieces, and more. It is organic and alive, always changing and evolving."

Creating this zoo was a collaborative effort. "I did a lot of the work on it, but sometimes the kids would help me. I built a brick path, and I said we could build exhibits around it. Different kids would come by and set up exhibits. Lucy set up the exhibit with the zebras."

Lucy is an interesting case study for how the N Street community raises children. Hammann, the adoptive mother who was feeding her when I visited in late 2007, died of cancer in 2009.[1]

When she became ill, Hammann prepared the community and Lucy for her death. Wolf and Cloud became Lucy's legal guardians. Lucy began spending some nights at the Wolf-Cloud house months before Hammann died. Hammann gave every home in the community a refrigerator magnet with Lucy's smiling face to remind them to keep an eye out for her.

Lucy is 4 now, and both she and her life in the community are blossoming. Wolf and Cloud officially adopted her, and they are solidly in charge of her upbringing, but many other adults are highly involved with her as well. She often helps Walker with gardening or the Plastic Fantastic Zoo. Eric Jensen, a stay-at-home father of 10-month-old Anders, takes her to ballet. Stuart Robinson, an old friend of Hammann who developed a close relationship with Lucy from the time she arrived there from China, takes her to Chinese class.

And of course, she frequently plays with other kids there. She jumps on the trampoline and swings in the backyard with kids named River and Granite. She also takes on the role of big sister with Anders, who comes by her house every morning for breakfast with his father.

Even at the tender age of 4, it's quite apparent that Lucy is a charismatic, confident, social little girl. Wolf says, "She'll go on her own to a number of other people's houses. 'Bye!' and off she'll go."

It's not just the young children who reap the benefits from the extended community. Although the teenage years are typically a time when children make efforts to break away from their families, spending time with friends far from home, N Street teens are different. First, because of the communal nature of the place, teens can immerse themselves in deep social interactions that are separate from their parents, but just a few feet away. Second, unlike other teens who focus almost exclusively

Lucy plays with a friend at a water fountain in the N Street backyard.

on peers their own age, N Street teens have significant relationships with adults in the community.

Bonding between all kids and adults at N Street solidifies through the many rituals and traditions that have evolved here. There are celebrations for Dia de los Muertos (Day of the Dead) and Solkwahamas (winter holidays), a holiday gift exchange, an Easter egg hunt, and a Coming-of-Age Celebration. The latter is one of the most unique rituals, designed to make 16-year-olds reflect upon what they would like to get rid of from their childhood and what they'd like to keep. The honoree chooses a few nonparent adults to plan the celebration, deepening his ties with those adults in the community; after this celebration, he can be part of the adult events, included in discussions and decisions, and expected to take on more responsibility like cleaning the chicken coop or doing yard work. "One of the best parts of growing up there was having adult friends," said Wolf-Cloud. "I really think that had a huge impact on who I turned out to be."

Bringing Cohousing Ideals to Your Street

Although there are few true cohousing communities in the Unites States (look at cohousing.org for a directory), residents of any neighborhood can take steps to emulate what appeals to them about N Street.

Hold regular common dinners: When's the last time you had your neighbors over for a meal? Try weekly or biweekly dinners hosted by one household and rotating throughout the neighborhood. See each other's houses, try new dishes, share recipes, and enjoy a night off from cooking—all while your kids play outside after.

Tear down fences: Pull your neighborhood together by sharing yards. If this idea makes certain people nervous, agree to save the wood after dismantling so that the fence can be resurrected if necessary.

Get involved in home sales & rentals: Invest in your neighborhood by attracting the right people to it: community-minded families with children. When neighbor homes are for sale or rent, go beyond telling your friends. Talk to the real estate agent early, post it on parenting discussion groups online, and make sure kids are playing outside on open house days.

Create rituals: Simple get-togethers that happen throughout the year can make your neighborhood feel more like a family. Think about organizing regular egg hunts, Halloween parties, joint birthday celebrations, gift exchanges, even a simple Super Bowl party. Host a neighborhood cleanup or gardening day where everyone gets outside and works together. It doesn't have to be elaborate.

Buy a house and convert it to a common house: It's a long shot, but if one neighbor or group of neighbors has the means, purchasing one house and renting it back to the neighborhood as a common house would be a wonderful feat. Kevin Wolf owns N Street's common house, but he also earns income from renters on the common house's second floor, and N Street pays him some nominal rent for the common house.

Dibble Avenue: Seattle
Frank the Builder Builds Community

Frank Shields is a builder—in more ways than one.

He's largely responsible for building an extraordinary culture on his block over the past 20-plus years using a combination of friendliness, fearlessness, wood, nails, a power saw, and Visqueen.

You see, when he's away from his block working, Shields is a contractor, and Visqueen is one of the common tools of his trade.

I'd never heard of it when I first talked to Frank about his Dibble Avenue block, between 75th and 77th in the Ballard neighborhood of Seattle.

"Uh . . . Vis-uhhh. Do you mean plastic?" I asked.

"Yeah, OK, plastic," he replied.

It turns out that Visqueen, otherwise known as polyethylene, is pretty darned important to the vitality of Dibble Avenue. Shields orchestrates the building of a waterslide for a two-day festival on Dibble every August, called "Nibble at Dibble."

It's a massive structure. The slide itself is three stories high and empties into a 5-foot-deep pool. Both the slide and the pool are lined in Visqueen. Frank created the design, procures the materials, and oversees its construction by numerous neighbor volunteers. At the end of the event, they disassemble it, so they have to reassemble it again every year. "There's nowhere to store it," Frank said. "The whole structure is probably 100 feet long. It can't fit in anyone's backyard."

It looks really fun—and really scary, which made me wonder if there'd been safety complaints.

"Oh yeah, the city has been after us to shut it down," Shields replied. "I really don't worry about it too much at all, honestly. They wouldn't want to fight with me

Frank Shields takes the plunge down the waterslide as some Dibble kids look on.

because they'd get a good fight." He added, "No one's ever gotten injured on the slide because we always have one adult supervising at the top and another in the pool."

The only thing that can shut down the Nibble at Dibble waterslide, as it turns out, is Shields himself. He injured his leg a few days before the event last year, so the slide was not built for the first time since the event started 21 years ago.

Nibble at Dibble was still a great party, with a potluck brunch and dinner, a bouncy house, a small inflatable waterslide for little kids, a dunking booth, an outdoor movie, and a pudding eating contest. And, regardless of what happens to his leg and the slide next year, Dibble Avenue will continue to be a remarkably vibrant place.

That's because Dibble Avenue's culture is a lot more pervasive than that of other blocks that run block parties every year. The neighbors here bond all summer. "Every June, right after school lets out, we have a camping trip two hours away, and 45 to 50 people from the block come," Shields said.

Then, for the rest of the summer, every few Sundays, they have a barbecue in front of Shields' house. Neighbors wheel their gas grills out to the sidewalk to cook, and when they eat, they sit at a couple of picnic tables that reside in the traffic strip (actually city property).

Outside of these summer events, the culture on Dibble is consistently warm and fun, especially for kids. Pretty much any day when school's not in session and it's not raining heavily, kids can be found playing in front yards. Some might be at the traffic strip in front of Shields' house, next to the picnic tables, where he installed a slide and some rope swings in a cherry tree.

Or, they may be down the street a bit on a Wiffle ball field that spans a couple of yards. Wendy Blake lives on that part of the block. For the parents like her who actively participate in the Dibble community, Blake describes the unwritten rule as "I'll watch out for your kids, you watch out for my kids." If a kid scrapes his knee outside, whether we have a kid or not, we're going to run outside and see if that kid's OK."

That mentality has its roots 15 years ago, before Blake and her family moved to Dibble. That's when Frank Shields' wife, Katie, woke up one morning with a severe neurological condition that left her paralyzed, and she spent more than a year in hospitals recovering and learning how to deal with her new condition. Three neighbor families who had kids around the same age as their kids, who were 6 and 9 at the time, pitched in to hold that family together in their mother's absence.

They cleaned and washed clothes at the Shields' house, they cooked for Frank and the boys, and they took the kids to practically all their activities. "They enabled me to continue working and spend a lot of time with Katie in the hospital," said Shields. "That experience really made our block much closer."

Even though their children are grown up now, the super-friendly, kid-centric culture at Dibble Avenue continues. Besides having a thriving play culture for older kids, Dibble Avenue continues to be a great place for new families with preschoolers. Blake notes, "When people who have toddlers move onto our block, oh my God, they are so happy to be able to take their toddlers outside and strike up a conversation with three or four neighbors who might be walking by."

When Blake and her husband bought their house there eight years ago, the block had quite a reputation in Seattle among realtors. Their real estate agent exclaimed, "Oh, Dibble! Everyone wants to live on Dibble!"

Actually, that's not quite true. One family that moved in next to the Shields' house a few years ago moved out after a year because they couldn't tolerate neighbors outside their house talking all the time. Other families that aren't interested in joining the "in-group" don't leave as fast, but they definitely exist. Blake estimates that roughly one-third of families there don't participate in neighborhood events.

The block's culture does have unspoken limits that prevent it from becoming "too close and too creepy," to use Blake's words. Pretty much all the activity happens outside, not inside, people's houses. "You don't find people knocking on each other's doors and bringing casseroles and saying 'Hey, why don't we sit in your living room all day?'" she said. "It's very much, 'If you want to join us in the public areas, we're happy to have you in our group.' People who take us up on that generally find that we're not about invading your space and telling you how to live."

I don't know about you, but I'd join them.

CHAPTER 10

Iris Way: Palo Alto, Calif.
A Neighborhood Summer Camp

To those of us who think of childhood summers as carefree times for neighborhood fun, free of schedules and direct adult authority, most children have no summers anymore.

Sure, school still ends every June and the weather still gets hot (except in San Francisco!), but neighborhoods are no longer filled with children's yelps and laughter on summer days. In fact, for the most part, neighborhoods are completely dead, as dead as they are during school days in the winter. Instead of going outside to play on their own, most kids either stay inside in front of screens, attend adult-run summer camps and classes outside their neighborhoods, or go on family vacations.

Of all the unfortunate aspects of childhood in 21st-century America, this fact depresses me more than anything else.

The American tradition of summer vacation began in the late 19th century, when families' lives were very different. Back then, virtually all mothers stayed home and children had a great deal of freedom. Today, most mothers work, and even if they're not working, they'd rather not stay at home all day. In addition, children have far less freedom in summer than they had decades ago. An indication of how times have changed is the U.S. Census Bureau research publication titled "Who's Minding the Kids? Child Care Arrangements: Spring 2005/Summer 2006."[1] Back when the summer vacation tradition began more than 100 years ago, no one would even ask, "Who's minding the kids?" Kids, even older toddlers, minded themselves outside in their neighborhoods, only coming home to get meals.

But today, most parents today find this tradition problematic. In most families, both parents have to work and that means they need to schedule care for their kids, often in the form of full-day summer "camps." If one parent is home, even part time, they feel compelled to keep their kids busy—after all, that's what all the other parents are doing. So they fill the child's free time with lessons and classes, or schedule playdates around town. All the planning for these camps and activities takes a lot of parents' time in the winter and spring. Then, in the summer, the logistics of dropping off and picking up kids at a different camp or activity every week or two can be quite a challenge—not to mention an exorbitant expense.

Jennifer Antonow and Diana Nemet of Palo Alto, Calif., are two moms who decided to bring back summers of play in their neighborhood. To kick every summer off, they run a weeklong neighborhood summer camp that is both very ambitious and very successful. They call it Camp Iris Way (hereafter referred to as CIW) after the main street in their small neighborhood.[2]

Antonow and Nemet wanted an alternative to professionally run summer camps for kids in their neighborhood, which cost a fortune, are booked months in advance, and do nothing to promote neighborhood friendships. They had a vision of a summer

A sign blocks cars as campers, counselors, and volunteer parents gather in the background.

of free play right outside their front doors, as they remembered growing up. And they believed that if they kicked it off by creating a "play camp" on their own street during an early week in summer, kids would take up the cause and be inspired to create their own fun during the weeks that followed.

They knew they had to get community support first. Their first e-mail plus numerous face-to-face conversations got overwhelmingly positive response. It seemed that parents of almost all young children in the neighborhood—in the dozens—were interested. Forty-three children ended up attending, 13 as counselors and 30 as campers. Antonow and Nemet were both thrilled and intimidated. They realized that they had an opportunity to make a big impact on their neighborhood, but they had to grope for ideas on how to run such a large neighborhood summer camp.

Key Decisions

The planning steps they then made were, for the most part, spot-on. Below are some key decisions they made in developing a successful camp for dozens of kids.

Recruit counselors: In my childhood neighborhood, adults hardly ever played with us young kids. Instead, we learned all sorts of games, as well as all sorts of moral lessons, from the older kids. Antonow and Nemet knew that older kids wouldn't be interested in attending a play camp aimed at younger kids as campers, so they got them to participate in CIW as counselors or counselors-in-training. Counselors were given ownership for planning activities and snacks, and were paid a nominal fee.

Recruit parent volunteers: Parents filled roles of banker, snack coordinator, photographer, first aid point person, and equipment manager.

Have a flexible location: CIW was like a Bedouin tribe, moving to a different two- or three-house-long section of Iris Way every day. This spreads out the burden of hosting it to different families and yards, and it also gives children an opportunity to spend some time on either their home turf, or the familiar turf of a close friend.

Have lots of fun props on hand: There's always dead time at some point during the day, or a camper who doesn't want to participate in an activity, so it's great to have a sandbox around for a 3-year-old and a basketball hoop with ball for older kids. "Oobleck," a mixture of two parts cornstarch and one part water, was one of their most popular props.

Plan an artifact: A piece of camp memorabilia that children create together can inspire neighborhood spirit throughout the year. For CIW, it was tie-dye T-shirts

Kids really went wild with the oobleck. The street looks bad here, but fortunately, oobleck washes off rather easily.

the kids could keep. It could also be a shared mural or mosaic, friendship bracelets, or even a DVD of camp highlights and campers' personal messages that everyone can take home.

With a good structure in place, CIW was ready to roll. The camp offered different activities each day, including a scavenger hunt, street hockey, water balloon battles, and art projects. Throughout, the goal was always to get kids to work together and explore the neighborhood in a new way. The finale was a neighborhood block party. Recalls Nemet, "It was a total neighborhood outpouring of love! Everyone was there. It was a billion times better to have a block party after an event like that than to have a regular block party."

Impact on the Neighborhood

"One of our biggest goals for doing this was changing the culture of the neighborhood," said Antonow. Specifically, the aim was to set in motion a culture of abundant free play, every day, that would carry through the rest of the summer and beyond.

By that standard, CIW did not completely succeed. "It was stark the next week, like a ghost town, because my kids weren't in other camps and everyone else's kids were," said Antonow. She has been mulling over ideas to instill this free play culture more deeply into Iris Way. One is to request to parents that they not sign up their children for camps the week following CIW. Another is to articulate a "neighborhood bill of rights" so that parents can share a common understanding about how kids can roam the neighborhood safely without having to check in with their parents frequently. "I just feel like there's social anxiety about what's acceptable and what's not," she says.

Still, Antonow adds, "I do feel like we got somewhere. We definitely made progress. There are more friendships. I was particularly happy to see a lot of multiage friendships develop. More families know one another. I heard people say, 'I feel so much more comfortable borrowing a cup of sugar.' And I think that's progress, I really do."

Nemet concurs, noting that she was particularly happy with the new friendships she saw. During the week after the camp, her fifth-grade daughter played a lot with a kindergartener and a third-grader she had come to know better. To a lesser extent, those relationships endure today. "I never would have expected that, but it's great."

Perhaps the most encouraging sign that that first year of CIW was successful is that they got almost unanimous participation of neighborhood kids when they ran it the second time in the summer of 2011. CIW had 72 kids, including 41 participants (from age 4 to third grade), 11 counselors-in-training (fourth- and fifth-graders), and 20 counselors (sixth grade through 12th grade). That's more than 90 percent of all kids between age 4 and 12th grade in the neighborhood!

Running a Small Neighborhood Summer Camp

My neighborhood summer camp, Camp Yale, is much smaller than CIW. It had just eight kids when I started it in 2009, and although it's grown every year, it still had fewer than 20 kids in 2011. I wish it could have the impact on our neighborhood that CIW has had on theirs, but I'm still very pleased with it. From my experience, here are what I consider to be the bare bones essentials you need to run a camp for 10 kids or fewer:

Plan one fun activity each day: Ideally, kids can just get together and play with no supervision, but if that were happening, you wouldn't be contemplating running a camp, right? The activity on the first day is particularly crucial, and the planned activity diminishes in importance with each day, but it's best to have a daily activity planned before camp starts. Plan on it taking up roughly half the time of the camp day, or perhaps a bit more. If things go well, kids will be playing on their own by the end of each day.

Let spontaneous play take over: If they kids are playing very well on their own, by all means, step back and let them go. Allowing that kind of play to flourish is far

Kids at Camp Yale end up bonding a lot, regardless of whether they knew each other before, because of the small number of children there.

more important than any plan you might have for the day. I've ignored part or all of the daily plan at Camp Yale many times, and I've never regretted this.

Have one home base: Moving around the camp site day after day can be very labor intensive, and besides, if you keep it in one place, you can accumulate lots of props for kids to play with.

Get lots of props: This is as important for a small camp as it is for a large one. You'll never have all kids paying attention at every activity, even in a small camp, so you need fun playthings laying around.

Have at least one leader who's there every day: A total handoff from one parent to another won't work. At least one parent should be there every day to provide continuity. Of course, that leader need not lead the particular activity every day.

Have a stable group of kids: At least half the kids, preferably all, should come every day. The impact of a few drop-in campers is bigger on a small camp. Group instability harms the process of group bonding that usually happens over the course of the camp.

PART THREE

How Can I Solve This Problem?

Practical ways to get involved and foster free play in your neighborhood—starting now.

Move to a Potential Playborhood

Does moving seem like a radical notion to combat the free play problem? Maybe, but maybe not. Practically all of us will move homes at least once when our children are young. In fact, U.S. Census Department statistics say that about one in six families with young children moves every year.[1] To put it another way, the average family will move about two times between the birth of the first child and the time that first child reaches the teenage years. Why do we do it? Almost invariably, one reason we give is that we're moving to make a better life for our kids. Unfortunately, whether the new home we move into is better or worse for our kids is a crapshoot because we typically don't search for the attributes of a home that kids care most about.

Take my story. In 1974, when I was in seventh grade, my family moved from our house on Rose Leaf Road in suburban Pittsburgh to a larger, more luxurious home a couple of blocks away on Stancey Road. Any real estate agent or knowledgeable home buyer would look at those two houses and agree with my parents that the Stancey house was better than the Rose Leaf house. It had larger rooms and more of them. It had a more open layout. It was constructed better. It had better "finishes." The Stancey house was also a "good buy." It was surrounded by houses of even higher value, and the development in which it was situated was newer and trendier.

Unfortunately, none of those things mattered to me. The Stancey house was absolutely, positively worse from my point of view. You see, the block that the Rose Leaf house was on was full of kids who played outside almost every day. The Stancey house block had a number of kids around my age, but fewer of them. The main problem, though, was that they didn't play outside. Stancey just wasn't a "community" the way Rose Leaf was. I easily could have walked the short distance up the hill to my old Rose Leaf neighborhood, but I was too lame. Instead, I ended up sitting in the big family room watching TV every afternoon after school, eating saltine crackers and drinking soda.

This experience taught me that what kids value in a home has little, if anything, in common with what parents usually value. Fundamentally, kids value the neighborhood around the house and parents value the house itself. The yard is one thing they both seem to value somewhat, but they usually have very different opinions on how it should be used.

Many parents today might argue that their kids care a lot about internal house features like their own bedroom or their house's family room. I would argue that in most of these cases, kids care about these features because they have never lived in a house whose neighborhood was alive with kids. At the Stancey house, I cared a lot about our family room because I spent a ton of time there. However, because I had grown up on Rose Leaf Road, I never thought our family room was more important than a vibrant neighborhood. Most kids today have never experienced a neighborhood like I had at Rose Leaf, so they have no idea of the positive impact it can have on their lives.

Interestingly, back in the 1970s, a family moving had to be pretty unlucky to not land in a Playborhood. We were unlucky at Stancey. Today, though, it's the opposite. A family moving would be extremely lucky to move to a Playborhood because they have all but vanished from American society. Moving to a *potential* Playborhood—a block that has all the raw ingredients for a Playborhood, such as lots of children and a calm street, but doesn't have children playing outside in groups frequently—is feasible for families today, but it still takes a lot of searching. This chapter will help you achieve this goal.

Before going on, I'll make a distinction between a block and a neighborhood. The term "neighborhood" is an amorphous term that can span from one block to dozens or even hundreds of blocks. The Random House Dictionary defines a neighborhood as "the area or region around or near some place or thing."[2] This definition could imply anything from a block to a small town. Because the block is the fundamental range for young children in America to roam on their own, I will most often mention the block when discussing the search for a potential Playborhood around a home for sale.

Renting or Buying in Multi-Unit Buildings

The recommendations in this chapter come from my experience searching to buy a single-family home, so it does not specifically address the searching process for rentals or for homes in a multi-unit building (condos or apartments). Nonetheless, most of what's in here is very applicable to these searches. All children need neighborhood play, regardless of where they live. Thus, all parents need to pay very close attention to the immediate area around a home in order to make a good choice for their kids.

Renters, in general, expect to live in a home for a shorter period of time than do buyers, so they can't justify spending as much time searching as buyers. However, I still recommend that they reallocate much of their search time from interior details to the neighborhood variables that I discuss in this chapter (see "Seven Indicators of a Potential Playborhood" below).

Seekers of homes in multi-unit buildings need to focus on the residents of the buildings they're considering, rather than residents of houses on a block. In fact, because the units in a building are so much closer to each other than are single-family homes on a block, immediate neighbors are that much more important. It may feel a bit awkward at first knocking on the doors of units in a potential building, but the information you'll get will be extremely valuable. Sure, you might get a cold response or two (or three), but ask yourself, wouldn't you rather live in a building that has friendly neighbors who are interested in meeting you?

My points about investigating the outdoor environment are still vital. Kids still need calm streets, walkable destinations, and good schools. However, one very important "bonus" that many multi-unit complexes provide is common space adjacent to buildings, like a courtyard. You should investigate any shared space personally and ask neighbors about their use of it. Common spaces between buildings are often ideal places for "neighborhood hangout." In Chapter 12 I describe one apartment courtyard that serves as a great hangout for a half-dozen toddlers and their moms.

Seven Indicators of a Potential Playborhood

If you see large groups of kids playing as you drive down a street, by all means write down where you are so you can search for homes for sale there. But in general, when you visit a block with a home for sale, it's far more likely that you'll see *potential* for vibrant neighborhood play than the real thing. Below are seven indicators of a potential Playborhood that you should look for on these visits.

Kids

Whenever a moving truck pulled up to a house to move in a new family on our block when I was a kid, we'd ask the same three questions: a) Do they have kids? b) What ages? and c) Boys or girls? That's all we cared about. We wanted kids of the same gender as us (this is before puberty!) and the same age. The presence of children on a block is the most important "raw material" for a Playborhood. One child around the same age as each of your kids is good, but obviously, many children around the age of each child is better. Large group play is qualitatively different from small group play, and in many ways, it's better for children. Another important point is that kids next door are much more valuable than kids on the other end of the block. Many parents have told me that the fact that their next-door neighbor has kids their kids' ages is the single most important reason they're happy to live where they do.

Outdoor Life

Any sign of strolling or outdoor socializing on a block is an encouraging signal, whether those neighbors are children or adults. Parents who spend time outside in the neighborhood likely have children who do, too. Also, adults outside mean that there are likely to be "eyes on the street," providing a safer environment for kids. If you hear about special events like block parties held there or festive Halloween displays for trick-or-treaters, that's great, too.

Of course, it's great to see children actually playing outside, but not all "play sightings" are equal. The more kids are playing, and the more intense the play, the better. Six kids playing a pickup game of basketball or building and decorating a playhouse is much better than two kids playing catch or coloring with sidewalk chalk. Not only do large groups and intense play often lead to more fun for the participants, but they also indicate that the children there have more of a commitment to playing there often.

Families who have kids often leave kid debris right in the front of their house.

Kid Debris

Not even in the best Playborhood are kids playing outside at every possible moment, but those who do so often leave physical evidence behind. This "kid debris" is an indirect way of observing the first two Playborhood indicators, kids and outdoor life. Kid debris can be in the form of structures that parents have installed for kids, movable stuff that kids or parents left behind recently, sports gear, bikes and trikes, artwork that children have created such as murals or sidewalk chalk drawings, or car seats. Study the nature of the kid debris to guess the approximate age of children there. For instance, a stroller on the porch indicates a baby. Bikes of different sizes belong to kids big enough to ride them.

Calm Streets

Automobile traffic destroys neighbor relations. That's the conclusion of a landmark study conducted in the late 1960s and early '70s by Donald Appleyard. He studied the relationship between street traffic and neighbor relations on three adjacent blocks in San Francisco.[3] Table 1 on the following page lists each street, showing the traffic volume and residents' average number of friends who lived on the street. The result is striking. Residents of Light Street had three times as many friends and two times as many acquaintances as did residents of Heavy Street.

	Vehicles per Day	Friends per Person	Acquaintances per Person
Light Street	2,000	3.0	6.3
Medium Street	8,000	1.3	4.1
Heavy Street	16,000	0.9	3.1

Appleyard didn't measure children's outdoor play activity on these streets, but it's obvious that the busyness of a street has a dramatic negative effect on play. From children's point of view, the discounts that are offered for houses on busy streets aren't worth it. They're far better off in a smaller house on a calm street than in a bigger house on a busy street.

Walkability

If children walk and ride their bikes in their neighborhoods frequently, rather than always getting driven around by their parents, they are more likely to hang out there and play as well. It's important for kids to live in a house that has key walkable destinations such as an elementary school, a park, a food store, a branch library, and child-friendly retail shops or restaurants. The Waters' New Urbanist design standard of having key family-friendly destinations within a safe 10-minute walk, described in Chapter 6, is very difficult to find, but it's certainly a fine goal.

Walkability of the elementary school is by far the most important to a family, provided the family's children attend that school. Children who walk to elementary school are outside walking twice every day, and the leg home is often an opportunity to start some sort of play. Next important is an attractive park, preferably one that actually attracts children who roam on their own (though few do).

By a "walkable" destination, I mean that the walking route should be short enough and safe enough that parents will feel comfortable letting their children make the walk. "Short enough" depends on the age of the child and the taste of the parent, but less than one mile is a decent rule of thumb. Of course, closer is always better. As for safety, parents are most reluctant to let their children cross busy streets, and a crime-ridden block can also be a problem. So, a school that is one entirely safe mile away is probably more walkable than another that is half a mile away, but on the other side of a major street.

Another component of walkability is sidewalks. Sidewalks make walking safer. Of course, they don't make crossing streets any safer, so a sidewalk-lined route to school that crosses a busy street is still problematic. Still, they keep pedestrians off the street and make it easier for kids to run, ride bikes, and navigate scooters or roller skates away from cars.

At walkscore.com, you can obtain a "walk score"—a 0 to 100 score of walkability—for any address. This score measures distances of most common destinations (retail shops, banks, parks, schools, etc.) to that address. It provides a good first guess at the walkability of that place, but because it doesn't take into account the safety of walking routes, you shouldn't rely on walkscore.com completely.

Low Crime

Violent crime has been dropping in the United State for the past two decades, and its possibility is not a major concern for most neighborhoods. However, some low-income neighborhoods and blocks do pose a significant danger to their residents, especially to children. They also sometimes pose a danger for residents of neighboring areas, especially in large cities where neighborhood conditions change significantly from one block to the next.

If you do have some concern about a particular location, you can try to find crime statistics for a town or neighborhood online (try doing an Internet search for <neighborhood name> and "crime statistics"). I utilized such statistics when I lived in San Francisco. I found them somewhat useful, but the geographic areas defined in those statistics were much larger than I would have liked. Like neighborhood life, crime definitely varies block by block.

Also, by spending an hour or so in the evening, in a parked car watching the area right around the house you're interested in, you can learn a lot. The worst case is if you see a few people who don't look like they live there, and no residents. Second worst would be if no one is outside. If you see many residents around walking or chatting, this is the best case. That means they consider it safe enough to be outside at night. Also, their presence would likely scare off potential criminals.

Good School(s)

When children attend an elementary school in their neighborhood, their neighborhood lives are richer because they share their school lives with other neighbor children. Ideally, they walk to and from school together, and they form friendships with neighbor schoolmates that help them integrate their school lives with their home lives. Living close to an elementary school that's good for your children can be quite valuable.

What criteria should you use to determine whether the neighborhood school is a good school? A school's first job is teaching children academic skills well, so you must decide if the school is sufficiently strong academically. Most parents have come to use average standardized test scores of a school as a measure of its academic quality. One useful site for researching scores across schools is GreatSchools (greatschools.org).

You should definitely not stop there, though. Depending on who you talk to, test scores of a school are somewhere between slightly misleading at best and highly misleading at worst. I won't enter the debate here about how valuable test scores are to measure a school's ability to teach academic skills, but somehow, you need to figure out some method to determine whether a school is academically strong enough for your children.

Academics aren't the only thing that matter to parents, though. Besides demanding that schools demonstrate a great academic track record, we should demand that schools promote play at school and at home. During the school day, many schools have either severely reduced or eliminated recess. This not only deprives children of play, but it deprives them of learning opportunities as well. A 2009 study in the journal *Pediatrics* shows that children with more recess perform better in school.[4] The study does not differentiate between the effects of different types of recess on learning, but schools that highly restrict what children can do[5] at recess should also be avoided because this simply takes most of the fun out of it.

In addition, schools make play after school difficult when they assign large amounts of homework every night. As described in Chapter 2, American children's homework time increased from 1981 to 2003, and I suspect that it probably increased much more from 2003 to today. Meanwhile, educational researchers have not been able to find any relationship between homework in elementary school and academic achievement.[6] Obviously, this homework time eats into children's free time that they might otherwise use to play outside.

Realizing that homework is getting out of hand, many schools have begun to limit it. One of the many reasons my wife and I decided to move where we did is that the principal of the neighborhood school has mandated a "reduced homework" policy for his teachers,[7] even though the school's test scores indicate that it's keeping up with its more homework-heavy neighbors academically. Note that a movement affiliated with Stanford University's School of Education called Challenge Success (challengesuccess.org) runs seminars and conferences for educators to get schools to limit homework. Hundreds of schools have already begun implementing Challenge Success recommendations.

Can the Real Estate Industry Help?

My wife and I took two and a half years to find our present home in Menlo Park. That's a very long time. We were pretty intense about it, too. We never backed off the market for any period of time, and we never really readjusted our criteria.

Why did it take so long? From beginning to end, we stubbornly held on to the notion that a neighborhood for kids—what I now call a Playborhood—was our first priority. Other than price, all that stuff we saw on the real estate Web sites and multi-list reports was useless to us before we found a block we liked with a home available. Architectural style? Kitchen appliances and countertops? Whatever. Bedrooms, baths, and square footage? We may have had preferences for all those things, but they're *secondary*. None of these things can give our kids a good life like a Playborhood can.

Think of what it would be like to online date if your first criterion was looks, but there were no photos of prospective mates on the site. You'd waste an awful lot of time going on first dates with people you're absolutely not attracted to. You'd know it as soon as you walked into the café, but then it's too late. Another wasted hour. . .

That's analogous to what used to happen to my wife and me countless times when we went house hunting in the early stages of our search. We'd go to see houses that supposedly have "good neighborhoods," nice photos, the right numbers of bedrooms and baths, and a price in our range, only to discover almost every time that the block would be dead boring for our kids. At the rate we were going then, we'd never find a house we wanted in a potential Playborhood.

If we just went with the flow and searched for a home the way families and real estate agents normally do, focusing completely on house attributes and school district, we'd be as likely to end up in a dull and lifeless neighborhood as if we put on a blindfold and threw a dart at a map: a 90-plus percent probability in most areas. So, we were bound and determined to not go with the flow. We wanted to find the available homes in the blocks with the most Playborhood potential *first*, before narrowing our search.

Our real estate agents tried hard to help us. They were quite knowledgeable about the overall market in our area of interest, but their industry failed them. It wasn't their fault. The kind of neighborhood information we were seeking—i.e., the "Seven Indicators of a Potential Playborhood" described in the previous section—is at a level of detail far deeper than what could be expected by a buy-side realtor. Recall that a buy-side real estate agent shows his or her client multiple homes per week.

Sellers definitely know the answers to all these questions, and they have an economic incentive to provide the information because it could increase the price of the home. In a survey on Playborhood.com, I found that about two-thirds of parents would move from their present home to an identical one in a nearby neighborhood that had significantly more opportunities for their children to play outside, and they would pay tens of thousands of dollars to make that change.[8] The best sell-side real estate agents pull this information together somehow, but they haven't been given the tools by their firms to record it and disseminate it in any systematic way. No multi-list or third-party real estate database enables searching on any variables interesting to families like the Potential Playborhood Indicators. Why is this?

Real estate companies in the United States claim that they are prohibited by Fair Housing laws[9] from volunteering facts about a home or neighborhood around a home that would favor one group over another. In a *New York Times* article titled "Questions Your Broker Can't Answer," broker Michele Kleier, president of Gumley Haft Kleier, says, "If a family with children wants to know if there are other children the same age in a building, we're supposed to say, 'You should stand outside the building between 2 and 5 p.m. and see who walks in.' But how do you say something like that with a straight face?"[10]

For the most part, the industry's fears of running afoul of Fair Housing laws are unfounded. A white paper I commissioned from Relman and Dane (relmanlaw.com), one of the foremost Fair Housing law firms in the United States, finds that almost everywhere in the country, real estate agents are not prohibited from providing factual information about neighborhood characteristics that are important to families with children.[11] Thus, agents can provide information for each home for sale on all the Playborhood indicators—if they choose to.

Imagine the ad below in a local parents' magazine:

Two things are striking about this ad: 1) it's *very* attractive to families with children like mine, and 2) one *never* sees an ad like this, despite the fact that it's all perfectly legal. Does that mean these homes don't exist? Absolutely not. My home's block is even better in terms of most Playborhood indicators, and I saw quite a few with a block as attractive as this one.

Some people might believe that publicizing the fact that a number of children live on a particular block and play outside there will cause a child predator to stalk that block. This fear is not well-founded. As I've mentioned before, child abductions by strangers are extremely rare. Besides, all one of these rare predators has to do to find hundreds of kids is go to a school when kids are being dismissed in the afternoon.

FAMILIES, CHECK OUT

123 Maple Street, Fruitvale!

This home's block has:

· more than a dozen young kids between 0 and 12

· kids' games at least once a week in front yards, driveways, and the street: capture the flag, hide-and-seek, basketball, street hockey, and kickball

· an active community of adults that runs two great block parties every summer plus a very festive Halloween block party

· a very calm street, averaging fewer than 200 cars per day, 20 per hour at peak time*

· walkable retail shopping in quaint downtown Fruitvale just 1/2 mile (10 minutes) away, a walk that crosses no major streets

· a woodsy park with creek just five blocks away

Estimate based on survey from June 2009

Children living here are eligible to go to Fruitvale Elementary School, three safe blocks away. This school boasts the following:

· test scores in the 85th percentile in the state

· one hour of recess for all grades, K-6

· a reduced homework policy, following Stanford University's Challenge Success Program

The house has:

· 2 bedrooms, 2 bathrooms

· 1,350 square feet

· completely renovated in 2002, open floor plan

$___,000

Playborhood Hunting

Over the course of our long search for a home in a potential Playborhood, we figured out a lot on our own. It was painful because we had to invent our own Playborhood hunting techniques. Fortunately for those of you reading this, you can benefit from our experience. Here are our three fundamental Playborhood hunting techniques as a series of sequential steps.

1) Find Homes in Neighborhoods with Good Reputations

From your real estate agent, or from numerous real estate Web sites, you can get lists of dozens of homes in an area in your price range with the right number of bedrooms and square footage. How do you start narrowing that list? Rather than looking at the house first, I suggest that you do research on the reputations of neighborhoods and pick ones that are your highest priority. Specifically, choose neighborhoods that have reputations for good Playborhood potential. Then, choose homes that fit your high-level criteria (price, bedrooms and baths, square footage, etc.) in those neighborhoods.

You can start by identifying good schools. You can get test score information from a site like GreatSchools.net. To get information on recess and homework policies, ask your real estate agent and parents who live in the various districts, read articles in the local newspaper, and, if it's the right time of year, attend public information sessions for parents of incoming kindergartners. These are very revealing of the general philosophy of a school, even if your child isn't entering kindergarten in the upcoming year.

Unfortunately, researching the other Playborhood potential indicators for a neighborhood is much more difficult. What you hear and read about neighborhood reputation is often not useful for determining if your children would have a great life there for two reasons: assessments are excessively vague and positive, and the size of the area being referred to is too large. I'll discuss each of these in turn.

Excessively vague and positive assessments

Accurate neighborhood reputations are not easy to find. Local newspaper reviews of neighborhoods tend to be uniformly positive and overgeneralized, as are real estate agents' statements about neighborhoods.

Even parent friends who live in a neighborhood you're interested in tend to give vague, uncritical assessments ("It's a great neighborhood for kids! We love it there!"), but at least they are *capable* of providing more detailed information with more prodding. In my home search, I learned to ask friends very specific questions like the following:

"Exactly where do you live?" ("I live in XYZ neighborhood" isn't specific enough.)

"Do your kids ever play outside on their own (unsupervised)? How about other kids? If they do, how often do they do this per week? At what age do they start? With how many kids?"

"Let's say I'm driving down your street one weekday afternoon at 4 p.m. What's the probability that I'll see kids playing in their front yards or on the street? How many might be playing there? What might they be doing?"

"Where do your kids' closest friends live?" (If none of their friends are within a block or two, that's not a good sign.)

"How safe is the street the house for sale is on? Do you let your kids ride bikes on it or cross it when you're not watching? If your kids are preschoolers, do you anticipate letting them do this in their elementary school years?"

Do kids walk to school in your neighborhood? What percentage, would you say? What ages? At what age do kids walk without parents?

Asking questions like these of parents who live in a neighborhood helps you get the "real scoop" on it. Ideally, you should ask multiple inhabitants of each neighborhood these questions because one person can often have some sort of bias. For instance, a parent of a child who goes to a private or magnet school 30 minutes away will have a different perspective from a parent of a child who walks every day to the neighborhood school.

The size of the area

Often when people talk about a "neighborhood," they're referring to a community of at least a dozen blocks, sometimes more than 100. So, discussions of a neighborhood's suitability for kids usually refers to a much larger area than what's most important to you. Take the following example. Let's say you have two kids, 4 and 7. A friend of yours with kids around the same age recommends the College Terrace neighborhood of Palo Alto, a neighborhood of a couple dozen blocks, as being great for kids' outdoor play. In fact, according to a profile of College Terrace in the local newspaper, it has many blocks where outdoor play happens, and your friend lives on one particular block like this.

Now you've just found out about a house for sale in College Terrace, many blocks from your friend, and you're considering making an offer on it. It caught your eye because it's in College Terrace and because it's *perfect* in all the conventional dimensions—price, bedroom and baths, square footage, architectural style, etc. Should you take the plunge?

Not yet. Absolutely, positively not yet. All that sounds good, but now you're ready to really find out whether the block this house is on has Playborhood potential. What if this house is on a block with nothing but empty nester couples and families with high school kids? Despite all the wonderful stuff about College Terrace in general, I say it's a big thumbs down. Your kids will not have great neighborhood play opportunities, regardless of how good the "neighborhood" is for kids.

Certainly, the reputation of College Terrace that you heard from your friend and the newspaper profile is valuable because they increase the probability of Playborhood potential. However, neighborhood reputation is nothing more than a crude screening device. To actually find the potential Playborhoods, you need to take the next steps in this section: research close neighbors online and walk and talk in the neighborhood.

2) Research Playborhood Indicators Online

Now you've culled a list of homes for sale in your target neighborhoods. Of course, these listings don't include any Playborhood indicators, so you're only getting information about price, address, bedroom and baths, square footage, photos, etc. Unless you're lucky enough to know someone who lives on or near the block of one of the homes on your list, all the information you have on the Playborhood potential of these homes is the neighborhood reputation information you've collected.

How do you further narrow down this large list of homes to those with the highest Playborhood potential? One thing you can easily do is examine an online map to see the street the house is on and what's around it. You can't see exactly what traffic will be like from a map, but sometimes it's obvious that the street is a main street. On the other end of the spectrum, if it's a cul-de-sac, you can bet it's a calm street. In addition, scan the map for facilities close to the house that are desirable (a park or school) or undesirable (a factory or a wastewater plant).

After narrowing down your list using online maps, you could just jump to the next step—"Walk and Talk on the Block"—for each home on your list. However, because driving to each home and nosing around there takes an awful lot of time, I've devised an online research method to try to learn about the neighbors immediately around the home for sale. It involves searching publicly available online information on these close neighbors first to get some indication of whether kids my kids' ages might be living there. This is only one potential Playborhood indicator, but it's perhaps the most important one. If I felt there was a decent chance that at least one kid my kids' ages lived in a close neighbor's house, I'd feel a lot more inclined to spend the time to visit the house and neighborhood to get more information. Conversely, if I felt pretty sure the occupants all around were senior citizens, I'd be disinclined to visit the house.

Be forewarned: the methods I describe here seem invasive, but I'm only suggesting you search publicly available information, and besides, you'd be doing it for a noble cause—to find neighborhood playmates for your kids.

Here's the process I used and recommend:

1) Enter the address of the home you're interested in on a Web site that shows parcel maps and addresses like Zillow.com. Identify the addresses of the neighboring lots.

2) Go to a Web site that sells information on owners and occupants of houses like Intelius.com and buy "property reports" on the close neighbor lots. You may want just reports on the next-door neighbors, which are most important, of course, or you may want to extend your search a bit further. When I did this research for myself on Intelius.com, these reports were fairly expensive ($15/each), but I expect this cost to drop as competition in this field of online research increases. In any event, Intelius.com offers steep volume discounts if you call them. The reports from Intelius.com can give four very useful pieces of information: a) the date of the last sale; b) the name of the present owner(s); c) the name of the present adult occupant(s); and, in some cases, d) the age of the present adult occupant(s). If b) and c) are different, that indicates that the occupant is a renter, and is less likely to stay in that house long term.

3) Do a Web search on the names retrieved in c)—or b) if c) is not available. On rare occasions, this Web search will result in a hit that indicates that the person is a parent (for example, that person is on the PTA page for XYZ Elementary

School). More often, though, if you get hits, one of them might help you guess that person's age (perhaps a LinkedIn profile that lists college graduation in 1993, which implies being born about 22 years before that, or 1971).

Of course, d) is a direct way to get the occupant's age, but it's often not available. Age of occupant is a decent indicator of whether children of a particular age live there. There are no rules, but, for instance, a 48-year-old woman is unlikely to have a baby living with her, but she may very well have an elementary, middle school, or high school student living with her. A woman or man 60 or older is unlikely to have any children residing there.

The age of the occupant plus a) together can serve as a fairly strong indication that kids live in the house. For instance, if the house has a male and/or female occupant about 35 years old, and if he or she just bought the house three years ago, it's likely that at least one preschooler lives there.

Lastly, a) by itself with no information on the age of the adult occupants is an indication of how old kids are, if they do indeed live there. For instance, someone who bought a house 15 years ago is unlikely to have preschoolers, but they may well have high schoolers. Someone who bought three years ago may very well have preschoolers, but they're much less likely to have high schoolers. Someone who bought 20 or more years ago is highly unlikely to have any children living there.

What you end up with in this research are probabilities that children of certain age ranges live in the homes of a few close neighbors. If you think there's a decent chance that there are at least one or more kids your kids' ages living in those homes, you have further qualified this home as the center of a potential Playborhood for your children.

In my home search, I knew I hit the jackpot when I researched the next-door neighbors of the home that I ended up buying. On one side was a man and woman who, I learned through a Google search on their names, had announced the birth of their daughter in a newspaper a year and a half earlier. The announcement noted that the newborn girl had an older brother. On the other side was a man in his 30s who had announced his recent marriage on his personal Web site about a year before. Most thirtysomething newlyweds who buy large suburban homes plan on filling them with kids. When I made my first visit to their house, I met his wife, who was seven months pregnant with a boy!

3) Walk and Talk on the Block

If all your research on the block around a home for sale gives you a pretty decent feeling that it may be in a potential Playborhood, and if you like the other conventional attributes of the house, you should visit to look around and talk to neighbors. After all, for getting a feeling for a block, there's no substitute for walking around and talking to neighbors in person. You shouldn't commit yourself to stepping inside the house the first time you visit there, or feel you have to wait for open house day. The information you got online gives you a pretty good idea of what you'll see inside. If the block is a strong potential Playborhood, then, and only then, should you step inside to see the interior of the house.

You should plan your visit for a time when you're most likely to see residents outside. If possible, go on a late afternoon with decent weather on a weekday or, better yet, a weekend. When you first get to the block, look for people outside. If you see kids your kids' ages playing, and if it looks like they've done that before, you've seen enough to qualify this house for an inside visit. However, you should still stick around and investigate the block more. Adults outside, or kids outside not playing, are also good signs.

Next, look closely for kid debris in front yards, driveways, front porches, and inside cars. Recall that the kid debris you see is not only an indication of whether kids live there and play outside, but also the ages of the kids who live there. If you see zero people outside and zero kid debris, you might just leave and write off the house because this quick scan can take less than five minutes. On the other hand, if you've found some reason to have a good feeling about the block, try to strike up a conversation with a neighbor there. You should first try to talk to someone who's outside, preferably a parent or a kid. If no one happens to be outside (not a great sign. . .), go to the house of the closest neighbor that has some kid debris in their yard and ring the doorbell.

To make contact with a neighbor, introduce yourself, saying something like the following, "Hi. My husband and I are interested in buying that house over there, and it's very important to us that our kids—__ years and __ years—play with other kids outside in the neighborhood wherever we move. Would you mind telling me what other kids live around here?" If the person is reluctant to answer, that's a bad sign.

You're interested in moving into a neighborhood with friendly people who want neighbors like you. In my experience doing this, almost all neighbors were very happy to tell me which houses had kids, and at what ages.

If the neighbor is friendly and forthcoming, try to get information on the other Playborhood indicators—outdoor life (kids' play + adult socializing), street traffic, walkability, and schools. You can use some of the questions I listed for asking about neighborhood reputation on page 111. Of course, make it a two-way conversation. Tell him or her about your family and why that block might be a fit for you. The neighbor should see that you have a sincere interest in the home and the block, and that you're an enthusiastic, friendly person looking for an enthusiastic, friendly neighborhood. In other words, this chat is an opportunity to see if you connect with that neighbor.

It's always good to get more than one point of view, so if you're sufficiently interested in that block and house, you should talk to at least one more neighbor.

If, after all this research, the block meets your minimum standard, try to get inside to see the house. However, note that once I started implementing this block-qualifying method, we didn't walk in to see 90 percent of the houses whose blocks I checked out. Thus, the few homes we walked through were already qualified by me as being on blocks with strong Playborhood potential.

Key Features of a Yard

Now that you've found potential Playborhoods with homes you might like, it's time to consider the yards. I make the yard a secondary consideration when you purchase a home not because it's unimportant, but because you can always change things about the yard on your own if you want to, but you can't change the potential Playborhood factors like number of children in the neighborhood, type of street, etc.

In the following chapter, I'll describe how to add a set of features to a yard to make it into a kids' hangout. Here, I'll describe three features of a yard to search for in buying an existing home: front porches and stoops, low or no fences, and kids' hangout features.

Front Porches and Stoops

Homebuilders practically ceased building front porches on homes in the latter half of the 20th century as population migrated out of middle-class urban areas in favor of new suburban tracts, with homes built for automobile access in front and leisure in back, often walled off behind fences. On the other hand, before the end of World War II, almost all homes had front porches and stoops.

Back then, porches and stoops were vital settings for American social life, deeply embedded in its cultural fabric. Families came out there every night after dinner to share gossip and community talk with neighbors.[12] My mother and father, raised in ethnic urban enclaves in New York and Pittsburgh in the 1930s and '40s, hung out most evenings on their front stoops playing cards, inventing imaginative games, or just chatting with neighbors. Countless courtships, from first formal meeting to marriage proposal, occurred on front porches. In fact, a study about how courtship in America changed over the 20th century is titled *From Front Porch to Back Seat: Courtship in Twentieth-Century America.*[13]

The porch was such a popular setting among Americans that four major-party presidential campaigns in the late 19th and early 20th centuries were literally conducted on the front porches of the candidates—James A. Garfield in 1880, Benjamin Harrison in 1888, William McKinley in 1896, and Warren Harding in 1920.[14] In other words, the candidates did not travel the country making campaign speeches, instead addressing the press daily from their porches. Three out of four times, this strategy worked, and the front porch campaigner was elected president.

Why were Americans of decades ago so enamored of porches? Researchers studying the impact of them on social life observe that they make certain social interactions possible.[15] A porch provides a zone that is in between the private domain of the home and the public domain of the street, a "transitional space." Thus, those on a porch can engage in many of the same activities that they would inside their house, but they do this in public view, so they are apt to engage in spontaneous conversations with passers-by. Those social meetings can be quite casual and open-ended. Also, parents can hang out comfortably on their porch while keeping an eye on their kids playing outside in the front yard.

Front porches have been making a strong comeback in new homes in the past two decades,[16] but a majority of homes for sale still have no porch. Plus, porches today are often attached to houses that are far from the street or sidewalk, so they are more private than public. Parents hanging out on a porch far off the street wouldn't be as able to strike up conversations with passers-by or see children outside of their own yard. In contrast, homes in New Urbanist communities like The Waters are right next to the sidewalk by design. Porches like these are best for promoting neighborhood life, and can be quite an asset for families.

Low or No Fences

Fences, particularly those that keep a child from seeing or accessing yards, severely restrict children's play in a neighborhood. In my childhood neighborhood in suburban Pittsburgh, there were no fences. When my sister and I went out to our swing set in the backyard of our corner house, kids from all over the neighborhood would often see us and walk over to join us. Backyards without any barriers at all between them served as long fields for football games or chase games like capture the flag.

Almost all backyards in the region I live in now, Northern California, are totally fenced in. Front yards usually have fences between them, and some even have fences or bushes separating them from the street. As a result, neighbor children have far fewer opportunities to play outside together. Certainly, children who have backyards can play there, but because they are fenced in, group play is far less likely than it was for the unfenced backyard of my childhood.

Look for houses that don't have fences, or minimal fences, if possible. Of course, some parents may prefer the privacy that fences bring, but this desire comes at the direct expense of children's play opportunities.

Kid-Friendly Features

Certain yard features are "kid magnets," meaning they draw kids there. Chapter 12 is devoted to telling you how to add a set of features in your yard to make it into a kid hangout. Most existing yards attached to homes for sale don't qualify as kid hangouts, but many have a feature or two that are attractive to kids.

Examples of these kid-friendly features are play structures, forts/playhouses, seating, sandboxes, trampolines, water features, or even good climbing trees, ideally accessible to neighbors.

My Playborhood Hunting Results

I succeeded in structuring my wife's and my home search to spend the most time on homes that were in potential Playborhoods. As a result, our present home on Yale Road is in probably the best potential Playborhood of all the homes we investigated.

Kids: It's surrounded by children our children's ages, about 12 between 0 and 6 within a two-house radius all around.

Outdoor life: Our block has a pretty high level of outdoor social and play activity, with, for instance, frequent street hockey games a few doors down from us and a large group of elementary school kids and their parents passing close by on their walk to school every morning.

Calm street: It's on an extremely calm street.

Walkability: It's within a half-mile walk to a supermarket, a three-quarter-of-a-mile walk to a nice retail area, and a very safe (but long) mile-and-a-half walk to the public elementary school.

Good school: Our public elementary school emphasizes more recess than its neighbors and limited homework, while remaining very competitive on academic quality as measured by standardized test scores.

Meanwhile, the house itself is good, but not great, in our opinion. It sits somewhere in the bottom half of the top 10 houses we visited in our home search, but it's absolutely clear that we made the right decision. Our boys could care less about the fact that the architectural style isn't "us," the banister on the main stairwell is cheesy, and the family room is very cramped. They would have liked to have a better yard, but obviously, we addressed this shortcoming since we've moved in.

Because we chose the best potential Playborhood and worked to improve the things we could after moving in, our boys are outside having fun pretty much every day from spring through fall, and a few days per week in the winter. Neighbor kids often join in. As I described in Chapter 3, the block's not quite a bona fide Playborhood yet because neighbor kids aren't playing outside together daily, but it's absolutely getting there.

Choosing Small-Town Life for the Family

"It's a place where kids never stop playing outside," Meagan Francis says of her small Midwestern town, St. Joseph, Mich. She claims that the probability of seeing kids playing outside in late afternoon in good weather is a startling 100 percent—and that partly fueled her decision to move here from Chicago five years ago.

Meagan, the author of parenting book *The Happiest Mom*, describes neighborhood life here as effortless. Certainly, it's not as vibrant as in small towns decades ago due to the same distractions kids have everywhere—video games, the Internet, and myriad structured activities. However, it's better than pretty much anywhere in cities or suburbs. People are relaxed and tight-knit and family oriented. It's the kind of life many of us dream about for our kids.

Meagan has five kids, 13, 11, 7, 5, and 2 1/2, and the first four roam their neighborhood fairly freely. The 13- and 11-year-old have few formal restrictions, but the town imposes its own natural limitations. "There aren't a lot of places you can go to in this town," notes Meagan. "Besides, my sister-in-law teaches at their middle school. She hears a lot from them there and gives me detailed reports."

This street corner in St. Joseph certainly looks the part of a charming, old-fashioned small town.

The 7- and 5-year-olds have good friends at a few nearby houses. One of these is three blocks away, and they're free to go there on their own. A simple text message to the other mom and they're off and running.

Meagan's street is a testament to how they facilitate kids' neighborhood play. In one family's front yard, there's a trampoline. In another, there's a kiddie pool. Kids are welcome to just drop by these yards and play. This inviting attitude extends to families without children as well. Meagan's next-door neighbors, who are retirees, let her kids and other neighbor kids play on their front yard anytime, without asking. "People around here aren't very protective of their space," says Meagan.

Parents are quite present every day in her neighborhood, creating a vibe that makes kids and parents very comfortable. "There are a lot of eyeballs around," she notes. "I see a lot of adults around during the day here, many with kids. There are a lot of stay-at-home moms, and a lot of days, I see work-at-home moms and dads. And I see lots of parents walking their kids and picking them up, even in the middle of the day for half-day kindergarten."

Meagan added, "Also, at 5 o'clock, everybody heads home from work. In the neighborhood we lived in in Chicago, parents didn't get home until 6 or 7 at night." So, kids got home later from daycare and activities, and there wasn't much time for kids to play around their yards and neighborhoods before they went to bed.

This sounds like a wonderful place for kids to grow up, doesn't it? So, what's the downside to living in St. Joseph? A big city like Chicago, besides being the home for millions of jobs, certainly offers many more interesting people, places, and things to do for adults.

"I find the lack of variety here is OK; you just get more creative with the way you have fun. Now, we invite people to our house more and we cook," says Meagan. "Or sometimes we just drive to Chicago [90 miles away]. It's not a big deal because we're only doing it once a month anyway.

"There's a misconception that all the interesting things to do are in the city," notes Meagan. "There are definitely more things to do, but not necessarily more quality things to do. More places to eat doesn't necessarily mean they're better. There's a time in your life when you want to experience everything and sample everything. But I'm totally OK just settling into the life we have now and making the most of it.

"I think the story for me," she adds, "is giving up on the idea that there's always something better around the corner. Living close to my brother's family and my good friend, and having a great life for my kids . . . that's really been worth giving up all that other stuff."

CHAPTER 12

Create a Neighborhood Hangout

Let's say you live in a house on a block with some Playborhood potential, so there are at least a few kids there your kids' ages, the street is somewhat calm, and it's fairly safe outside. Now comes the moment of truth: You persuade your daughter to tear herself away from the TV or the Wii or Facebook for a moment and peek outside to see if there's anything interesting going on.

What is she likely to see when she steps outside and walks down the block? Chances are, she won't see much that's interesting. She'd probably see a bunch of buildings and cars, and if she's in the suburbs or the country, she'd also see some trees, grass, and flowers. She may see some people, even a kid or two scattered about, riding a bike or pulling a wagon. Unless she's lucky or lives in a dense urban environment, she's very unlikely to encounter a park. To beat the TV or the Wii or Facebook, not to mention activities like dance classes or youth soccer games, your daughter needs to see something very compelling when she ventures outside. In other words, she needs to see something that, in her eyes, beats her alternatives.

The most likely thing to keep her outside is a gathering of children close to her age, but that's highly unlikely.

In this chapter, I'll explain the first step in making these gatherings a common occurrence in your neighborhood, so that your children and neighbor children will come to think of your block as a likely source of fun. In particular, I'll show how you can create a great kid gathering place, or hangout, in your neighborhood.

Why Kids Like Hangouts

Children of decades ago gravitated to places in their neighborhoods where they could find other kids playing. My father and his friends made a shack out of scrap metal and refuse from a junkyard in the back alley behind his house. This shack served as their social club, a home away from home that was a magnet for neighborhood kids. The back alley where this shack was located was a larger hangout space where my dad and his friends shot craps, played sports, and engaged in many other games.[1]

My childhood friends and I had a few hangouts, from the tree house in the woods where we hung out all summer to the stretch of street next to my house where we played all sorts of sports. Although we built the former ourselves, the latter was just a hundred or so feet of pavement and curb on which we painted bases for our softball games.

In *The Great Good Place*, Ray Oldenburg writes about "informal gathering places" for adults. He calls this a person's "Third Place" behind the first place, the home, and the second place, the workplace. People show up at their Third Place frequently and voluntarily, not on any schedule. They share informal, often humorous, conversations with friends and acquaintances there. The popularity of the late TV show *Cheers* is testimony to the fact that many of us yearn for a place like this outside of home and work where "everyone knows your name." Unfortunately, Third Places have all but disappeared from the lives of most American adults.

They have disappeared from the lives of children as well. Children's second place, their "workplace," is their school. Where has their Third Place gone? As with adults, Third Places for children should be informal gathering places, but for younger kids, they are more for active play than sedentary conversation. Still, it's vital to note that, starting around age 4 or 5, children want to play socially—*with* other kids, not alone. Increasingly, as kids get older, when they have some free time and consider what to do, they are more interested in *who* they can be with, rather than *what* they can do. Thus, what is most significant about hangouts for children is that, at certain times of day, they can just drop in there and almost always find someone else to hang out and have fun with.

A small proportion of children today have a sort of nomadic real-world hangout: the inside of their car, plus wherever their traveling sports team is playing. They practice close to home during the week, and travel hours away from home for games on weekends. Parents drive them to these events, often carpooling to share the driving burden. Because participating in these teams takes so much time, a great deal of bonding results between kids and between kids and parents, wherever they are. Unfortunately, the kids spend a great deal of this time strapped inside a car, and they spend practically all of it under the supervision of adults—both parents and coaches. In addition, the life of a traveling sports team is very disruptive to family life at home, particularly if the kid on the traveling team has any siblings.

For most children, online social networks fulfill their need for a hangout. Many tweens and practically all teens hang out on Facebook. In her article "Why Youth (Heart) Social Network Sites," Danah Boyd explains how teens' increased interest in online social networking is a direct result of their losing access to venues for real-world socializing. She writes, "The power that adults hold over youth . . . is the root of why teenagers are on MySpace in the first place."[2] Their behavior on these sites is quite analogous to what we adults of an older generation remember from our teenage hangout days:

> . . . they hang out, jockey for social status, work through how to present themselves, and take risks that will help them to assess the boundaries of the social world. They do so because they seek access to adult society. Their participation is deeply rooted in their desire to engage publicly. . .[3]

So, children of today haven't given up on "hanging out," they've just moved it from the real world to the road or online. Our challenge as parents is to create physical gathering places in our neighborhoods that will be more attractive than these alternatives.

Why Create Hangouts in Yards?

Kids of today must have a hangout within a block of their house, preferably in their own yard, or they won't have a neighborhood hangout at all. Most preschoolers these days are not permitted by their parents to roam outside their yard without a trusted adult watching over them. Many elementary school-aged kids have the same restrictions, and the ones who do get more freedom aren't allowed to roam more than a block from home on their own.

On the other hand, young children generations earlier were allowed to wander a mile or more on their own. When I was 4, I went with friends to the woods by our house, the place where we would later build our tree shack. Starting in first grade, friends and I walked more than a mile to elementary school every day. A poignant article in *The Daily Mail* chronicles how the roaming range of four generations of 8-year-old boys in one family in Sheffield, England diminished from six miles to 300 yards.[4] This is largely due to parents' fear for their safety.

Hanging Out When You Don't Have a Yard

Can you have a great hangout if you don't have a yard? Absolutely. In fact, if your home—an apartment, condo, or flat—is cramped, you might even be more likely to venture outside and be social. All you really need then is some decent common space and a few congenial neighbors.

Take the case of Jennifer Wagner and her kids.

"Back in Texas," she notes, "everyone our age we know who has kids has a house. It's much easier to buy a house there." They moved from Texas to Mountain View, Calif., where housing prices are much more expensive, two and a half years ago, for her husband's job.

Still, she's very happy living where she does. I can't argue with her. I visited the quaint courtyard of her apartment complex one summer afternoon. A half-dozen preschoolers were buzzing and laughing and crawling and running nonstop. Mostly, they were playing with a cardboard box. I was enthralled. Yes, I'd seen kids play with a cardboard box many times before, but I'd never seen so many kids play so enthusiastically for so long with such a simple thing. Jennifer told me that kids play like this in her courtyard almost every afternoon.

Three moms, Jennifer included, were around the courtyard, too, playing "tag team" with each other. One or two would go inside their apartments to get something done, and the remaining mom or moms would keep an eye on the kids. Clearly, everyone was very comfortable with each other.

On the way over to Jennifer's, I had just passed by an upscale suburban playground scene with a half-dozen or so individual kids playing independently, a disinterested nanny hovering over each one. Yawn . . . I'll bet they all came from nice houses with manicured lawns. My opinion? The kids at Jennifer's were much better off.

Jennifer and her neighbors have found the benefit in having apartments with modest amenities. "We have no air-conditioning, and our apartments are pretty small, anyway," she said. "The windows and walls are thin, but they let us hear friends playing, so we go outside."

She noted a couple of important factors that a complex should have to host a vibrant hangout space. First, a large common area that faces many front doors and welcomes all to join in, rather than feeling like it belongs to one unit or small section of the building. (Bonus points if the area is safe and well away from parking lots and streets; double bonus points if the area doesn't have any hazards for little kids, such as poisonous plants like the very popular oleander bushes.)

The kids at Wagner's apartment complex have a very active play life without much space or formal "play equipment."

Second, front porches are terrific, especially if you can put out a few folding chairs and some kid toys.

Jennifer also offered some suggestions on how to get to know neighbors well in a multi-unit building:

- Spend time in your common area. Go out there and let your kids play or eat picnics. Even if there's just a small patch of grass outside the front entry, be in it. Give people a chance to meet you casually.

- Start activities in the common area and invite neighbors out to participate: paint with water and brushes on concrete, make paper bag masks, turn cardboard boxes into houses, create baking soda and vinegar volcanoes, draw with sidewalk chalk, start a ring toss game.

- Host casual, drop-in parties inside your apartment. Knowing the inside of someone's home makes you much more comfortable with them.

- Give the neighbors a chance to know *all* the adults who live at your place, especially if you and/or your partner work during the day. Have tea or a cocktail on the front porch at night and be available for folks to say hi or chat.

- Create a signal so that young children know when they are welcome to knock and when they're not. For instance, closed front blinds can indicate a family isn't ready to entertain or be invited out.

- Keep at it. It takes months to build relationships.

Even with all the good activity in her building, Jennifer can foresee the day when she leaves her blinds closed there and moves out.

Frustrations with apartment living—from having to put away kid debris each day to having to cancel a courtyard party when the manager disapproved—will probably drive her and her husband to move out. But the irony is that if they buy a nice suburban house like their Texas friends, they may not be able to throw as fun a party there as they could now, in their quaint apartment courtyard.

"If and when we do move into a house, I hope we'll find a Playborhood like this one," Jennifer said. Alas, Playborhoods are rarely just waiting to be found, especially in single-family home neighborhoods, and it's an awful lot of work to create one. Jennifer's very fortunate to live where she does, even if she has no air-conditioning, thin walls, and can't throw an outdoor party. Honestly, if I were her, I don't know if I'd leave.

The current roaming range for children rules out most of the play settings previous generations of children took for granted. For instance, parks and playgrounds are often mentioned as the key venues to get kids outside playing,[5] but the vast majority of children do not live within a block of a park.

Decades ago, children didn't need their parents to make their hangouts—they created them for themselves or they lived in houses that had them already in the form of front porches and stoops. Kids today are different, though. Most of us will need to make our kids' hangouts in our yards for the following four reasons:

Kids Don't Have the Freedom to Be Resourceful or Imaginative

The wonderful children's book *Roxaboxen* tells the true story of a group of children who created a play village on a hill from rocks, sticks, and found objects. The kids laid out rocks in lines and rectangles to mark off streets and buildings. They used sticks for horses, which they "rode" in imaginary play. They used other sticks as spears for combat. They used round objects as steering wheels for cars.

The story resonates with the memories of many parents and grandparents who created similar make-believe worlds as children. Unfortunately, it is very difficult, if not impossible, to find analogous examples of children today being let loose in a big field every day for months like this. They rarely have the free space and time to improvise imaginative games with found objects, and the toys they play with leave very little, if anything, to the imagination.

Kids Don't Tinker

How do you anchor a tree house into two or three tree trunks many feet off the ground? What kind of ladder should be made to access it? What kind of railings should it have? There is no easy way to answer these questions—it takes a lot of thought and trial and error. Building a tree house takes days, if not weeks, of open-ended tinkering. On the other hand, children these days get instant gratification indoors when they engage in screen activities. Most of them just don't have the kind of time or attention span to build tree houses or forts, and if they did, they may not have access to the tools or basic skills they need to succeed.

Neighborhood Free Space Is Scarce

Vacant lots or woods like the place I frequented from the time I was 4 have largely disappeared from most neighborhoods. In addition, residential streets, where my father and I spent much of our childhood days, have become increasingly dominated by cars. Thus, our children's hangouts need to be in the only available space in our neighborhoods—yards close to ours. In fact, your own yard is preferable because it's most convenient for your kids and easiest for you to monitor.

Few Homes Have Front Porches or Stoops

Front porches and stoops were dominant features of homes in America until the suburban housing boom of the post-World War II era. Houses with them, if close to the street, have a built-in social gathering place. Unfortunately, most houses these days either don't have porches or are set back too far from the street to offer much socializing potential.

What About Lawsuits?

Parents who hear about my front and backyards often ask, "What about lawsuits?" In other words, to what extent am I concerned that a kid will get hurt on my property and that his or her parents will sue me for this, and how does this affect the features that I install and how I manage access?

Of course, parents should try to diminish the risk of accidents when they choose specific features. For example, in-ground trampolines like the one at my house are safer than the more common aboveground trampolines.

Another thing parents can do to mitigate the risk of a lawsuit is to get to know the neighbors who have children very well. In Chapter 14, I advocate that parents

"Make a Village," establishing close relationships with many neighbors. A neighbor mom who knows you and has hung out many times as her children play in your yard is much less likely to sue you than she would a relative stranger, regardless of what accident might happen.

Even after installing relatively safe features and establishing good relations with neighbors, parents who attempt to create a neighborhood kids' hangout still run a much greater risk of being sued than the owner of a yard in which no kid ever plays. Just kids' mere presence playing results in a significantly greater liability risk.

Do I think that additional risk is worth it for me? Absolutely. The probability that a child would get severely hurt in my yard, and that their parents, all of whom I know pretty well, would sue me for this is very, very small. I would venture to guess that parents who drive friends of their kids around in their car run a greater risk of getting into an accident and getting sued, but even this probability is quite small.

On the other hand, the probability that my kids will have a much better childhood because I've made it into a hangout is very high, close to 100 percent.

That's almost a 100 percent chance of a better childhood vs. a very, very small chance of getting sued. I'll take that deal anytime.

Characteristics of Kid Hangouts

Five characteristics of outdoor hangouts and their component features are fun, comfort, accessibility, visibility, and critical mass. I'll consider each of these below.

Fun

Naturally, children are drawn to things they consider fun. This is a very simple but powerful maxim. In deciding what features to put in your yard to attract children, you need to think like a child.

You should install features that appeal to children of diverse ages, even if you have one child, for three reasons: Neighbors with multiple children need to go to a place where all their children are engaged; your children will grow up, so their interests will evolve every year or two; and "age-mixed" play is good for all kids, so you should do what you can to encourage it.[6]

Ages 3 and Under

Young children up to 4 years old are most attracted by simple things that they enjoy manipulating with their hands like sand and water. At my house, our water fountain and sandbox are extremely popular with this age group. Most young children passing by simply cannot resist splashing their hands in our fountain. The sandbox is a bit less of an initial draw, but it holds children's attention longer. Some neighbor children visit it regularly and stay there for a half hour or more.

Ages 4-9

Children in this age group are more physical, expressive, and social. Thus, they are drawn to outdoor features that have one or more of the following characteristics:

Physical challenge: Many children at this age need to exercise rigorously and often, every day. Physically challenging features include play structures, sports equipment like a basketball hoop (at an appropriate height!) or a hockey goal, climbing challenges like fences or rock climbing toeholds on a wall, or jumping features like a trampoline.

In addition to features that have specific uses like a basketball hoop, active children also benefit greatly from open spaces with flat ground on which they can play various sports and games. For example, I've mentioned my smooth concrete driveway as being vastly superior to our old driveway with paver stones because my boys can scooter, skate, skateboard, bounce balls, play hockey, and draw with sidewalk chalk on it. Also, children are much more apt to run around and play on a field of grass than they are on a field of shrubs.

Outlet for creative expression: Features such as whiteboards, chalkboards, and easels can provide a venue for children to write messages and draw. A sturdy table and chairs can give children a workbench to build their creations. Outdoor storage or a shelf in a garage may be used to hold items for building things, from intricate, small items like beaded jewelry components to larger items that can be used to build structures.

Private domain: Structures like forts, playhouses, tents, etc. enable children to establish their own domain, and in some cases to create their own imaginary worlds. To give children a sense of ownership, it's best if they can create these structures themselves, but as I stated earlier, children these days don't usually have the resourcefulness to create a fort. To enable my children to build their own forts easily, I've given them a building set called Slotwood (slotwood.com). Slotwood is fabulous for creating life-sized structures, but

They're making a fort in my driveway using what I called "life-sized Lincoln Logs"—a product called "slotwood." (slotwood.com)

unfortunately, its particle board slats don't handle moisture well, so you can't leave Slotwood structures outside when it rains. Kerry Colburn, a mom in Seattle, takes an even easier route: She encourages her kids to make forts by draping sheets, old tarps, plastic or cloth tablecloths, or play parachutes over a picnic table, card table, or play structure in their backyard. Binder clips or clothespins for securing the fabric are always nearby in a plastic bin that kids can access themselves.

Ages 10-14

At this age, children are getting even more social, a trend that continues into the college years. They are also thoroughly immersed in digital technology. In fact, for many of these children, these two trends come together as they spend hours a day texting and on online social networks. We parents should try to accommodate these urges to socialize and to use technology, but in contrast to online social networks, we'd like our children to do these things in person, outdoors. Outdoor features that attract children in this age group include the following characteristics:

Private domain: This is a continuation of the same urge in children of the younger age group. Children at this age want even more independence. Before, hiding from others was a game. Now, keeping parents from seeing certain information and items is serious business. This is totally normal behavior from a child development point of view. Children today who don't have private spaces in the physical world are likely to shift these behaviors to the Internet, where they endeavor to keep their surfing and messaging private from their parents.

To satisfy this urge in the physical world for children of this age range, you need to provide a complete space or a compartment within a space that kids perceive as totally theirs. So, you might provide them with a shack or fort that they can lock themselves, or let them have a chest or box—inside a shack or elsewhere—that they can lock.

Digital technology: Beginning at this age range, if not before, children become heavy users of digital technology regardless of whatever restrictions parents try to impose. This is primarily due to the lure of three application categories: social networking, entertainment media (videos and music), and games. The media system inside the picnic bench in my front yard, which I mention in Chapter 3, enables us to play music and videos in an outdoor venue, thus making it a much "cooler" place for kids in this age group to hang out than it would be otherwise.

Comfort

Children have always valued comfortable features as part of their hangouts. For example, my dad's old shack had a roof overhead and old upholstered chairs and a potbellied stove inside. Today, when children are often accompanied by their parents or caregivers in their neighborhoods, comfortable features are even more important. These adults may stop at your yard if their kids are attracted to fun features you have there, but they're much more likely to stay awhile if they're comfortable.

So, what features add comfort to a hangout? First and foremost, seating is vital. Besides being comfortable (seat backs and cushions are good!), the seating should be situated so that the person sitting can see the kids playing. If it's situated close enough so that sitters and players can carry on a conversation, that's even better.

Second, the seating is more attractive if it's shaded from the sun, either by trees or by an umbrella or a roof. The picnic table in my front yard is shaded by a huge redwood tree.

Lastly, food and/or drinks can make people linger, and if you serve these, you should have some sort of table and seating so people can consume it comfortably. Recall from Chapter 6 that Share-It Square has a tea stand. That's a big draw for some neighbors to hang out there.

Accessibility

If neighbors and passers-by can't get to your yard, they won't hang out there. All barriers limit accessibility, but some do so more than others. A barrier with a gate is a lot more accessible than one without a gate. A barrier with an opening rather than a gate is even better.

Another aspect of accessibility is distance. A backyard with no fence around it may nonetheless be fairly inaccessible if it's far away from the neighbors you're trying to attract.

Visibility

Many people value privacy in their yards, but privacy is the enemy of community relations. A hangout must be clearly visible to neighbors and passers-by if you want to attract them. If a backyard is surrounded by a privacy fence with no gates, it's a poor choice for a hangout. At my house, we try to keep the gate to the backyard open at all times, and we also offer a ladder to kids who want to hop our backyard fence.

Front yards that have big fences or shrubs in front of them aren't ideal for hangouts, either. Some parents with small children say they like these front yard barriers because they want to prevent their children from running out into the street. I would suggest that they replace their privacy barriers with barriers that limit accessibility but not visibility, like a low picket fence.

Critical Mass

A yard that has one feature—a sandbox or a basketball hoop—will probably not become a bona fide hangout. Hangouts need a diverse collection of multiple features,

At The Waters, streets are the ultimate visible and accessible playspaces.

because kids get bored and want to try new things. You also want to account for siblings and for changing interests as years pass.

I don't mean to discourage parents who want to install a single feature in the yard. Something is surely better than nothing. However, think about what it would take for you to draw kids to your yard from the entire block and beyond on a regular basis. At any moment, at the least hint of boredom, they may run home and inside again, and they may never come back. And, once one kid stops coming by, others are more likely to stop as well. Yes, this is hard.

Plan It and Build It

I've shown why you should make your yard into a neighborhood hangout, and I've explained what characteristics that hangout should have. Now let's talk about the most important issues you'll encounter in making this happen.

Front-of-Home or Backyard?

Should you put your hangout in the front of your home (front yard, sidewalk, or street) or the back yard? Backyard community building is more consistent with the current American preference.[7] When you remove the fence between you and a neighbor and join yards, as N Street community members have done, you've only sacrificed your privacy to one family, not to everyone who walks or drives by your house. Besides, your children will stay far from the cars whizzing by at the front of your house. Of course, many families don't have a backyard, so this option isn't available to them.

Front-of-home community building has the potential to impact larger numbers of children and families. Because fronts of homes are viewable by the public, and backyards are not, renovations there can attract participation by many people, not just close neighbors.

I've chosen to add hangout features to both my front and backyards at Yale Road because I see the attractiveness of both venues. However, kids wander to my front yard features every day, but they visit the back far less often because they have to either scale our 7-foot privacy fence or walk the narrow pathway from our front yard to our backyard. When I installed our backyard features, I made a bet that I could get kids coming there on their own despite the obstacles.

Which Features to Include?

Choosing which features to include is more art than science. Within the guidelines I've mentioned, you still have a lot of options. You should make those choices first and foremost based on what will get your children out there and keep them there. They're the most important "customers" of your yard.

Also, choose at least some features that provide the opportunity for children to creatively customize them. If and when they paint their own designs, nail their own boards, or otherwise alter the features you provide, they'll develop a stronger attachment to them.

For instance, children should be able to customize their playhouse by drawing on the walls or adding features to it. The common plastic prefabricated playhouses make both of these difficult. Playhouses made of wood are better. Recall that the playhouse in my backyard is made of wood, and also I installed whiteboard on all internal walls to encourage drawing. Cardboard playhouses aren't permanent, but

At my front yard picnic table, kids wander over to play with our kids while we adults hang out and chat. Adult neighbors passing by often join us for a drink, too.

they can easily be pulled in and out of the house, and they're very easy for kids to customize.

How Much to Spend?

Every family's budget is different, so there is no one set formula for how much a family should spend on a hangout in its yard. However, I do have two things to say about how much a family should spend on its hangout space:

Focus on function: I have nothing against features that are aesthetically pleasing, but if you need to save money, focusing on function can save a lot of it. For instance, you can buy a new outdoor bench at an exclusive outdoor furniture store for $1,000-plus or buy a functionally equivalent used one at a garage sale for $20. You can spend thousands of dollars on a designer playhouse or put one together yourself (if you're handy enough!) with a couple hundred bucks worth of two-by-fours and plywood.

Emphasize outdoor features over furniture inside your house: Do your children care about the expensive couch in your living room? Those paintings on the wall? Do they care if you spend $2,000 or $200 on their bedroom set? Absolutely not. It's better for them if you save that $1,800 and renovate your front yard with that money.

Since we've moved into our house on Yale Road, my wife and I have made a conscious decision to spend virtually all our "upgrade" dollars on our yard rather than on furniture inside. That means we've purchased zero electronics, furniture, artwork, or rugs for the inside of our house, while we've purchased numerous amazing features for our front and backyards. As a result, our kids spend most of their free time, weather permitting, outside.

What About Theft or Vandalism?

Of course, if you leave play features outside, you risk that they will be stolen or vandalized. What should you do to address this risk?

Your first impulse might be to totally avoid leaving anything outside. However, people often overestimate this risk. At Yale Road and Share-It Square, very attractive features are left in front, clearly visible to the street, and theft or vandalism hasn't been a problem. This is particularly remarkable at Share-It Square because the features are on the sidewalk, not in a private yard, and because loose items like kids' toys are left outside at the Kids' Klubhouse.

Unfortunately, in many urban neighborhoods, theft and vandalism is too likely to risk leaving features outside. At Lyman Place's summer play street, Hetty Fox and her youth workers bring out all play features from a storage room every morning and put them away every night. This is a major issue there because it requires significant manpower every day.

My recommendation is to anchor down what you can, and test the limits of what loose features you can leave outside. If something gets stolen or vandalized soon after you start, you may decide to take away some vulnerable features. However, you may be surprised to find that your features survive well outside, unattended. If that's the case, you may want to put out a little more and see what happens.

Getting the Job Done

If you're merely buying a few preassembled features and have a good spot to place all of them, there isn't any "work" to be done to transform your yard into a neighborhood hangout. Otherwise, however, some work will have to be done, and you'll have to decide who will do it.

Assembly of purchased features: Some products are relatively simple to assemble, but some require a lot of work. For example, assembling a store-bought sandbox might require a screwdriver and an hour of simple assembly, whereas assembling a prefab playhouse like the one I purchased for my backyard might require a carpenter who has experience with framing and foundations. Play structures fall somewhere between these two extremes.

Of course, it's always good to save money by doing things yourself, but if you have the means, you may want to hire a professional (or a handy friend) to help with assembly of something new. Personally, I would have wasted the money I spent on my playhouse had I tried to put it up myself. We want it to remain structurally sound and weatherproof for years, and I couldn't even begin to assure that I could make this happen.

Landscaping: If you're installing a lot of features, you'll probably want to rearrange the existing items in your yard. N Street's common backyard has undergone landscaping changes pretty much every time a fence has gone down. Although houses still own their respective plots of land, the community has a common objective to connect all the plots. The stone pathway that weaves through every plot is the primary vehicle for connecting them all.

Dealing with local government: A lot of the changes you might imagine doing to your front or backyard may run afoul of your local planning department regulations. This is especially true of front yard renovations, which are usually more restricted than backyard renovations.

Mark Lakeman and his colleagues at Share-it-Square played a game of bureaucratic chess with a couple of departments in Portland city government for months before getting official approval. Initially, the painted mandala on the intersection pavement was a problem for the department of transportation, and the features on the corners violated regulations of the planning department.

My front yard project needed the approval of my city's building department. If I had tried to install a "fixed structure" like a playhouse or play structure in my front yard, or excavated below one foot for any reason, I would have had to ask for special permission. This may have required a public hearing.

My recommendation is to cooperate with local government processes and regulations, especially for places that are in plain view of neighbors like your front yard. If there's any hint that you may have a battle, check with all your close neighbors to get a sense of if they would support you in a public hearing. Without near-unanimous support from them, you will probably not win. Even if you have this support, "fighting city hall" will probably be quite time-consuming.

What to Do After You Build It

"If you build it, they will come" is the wrong attitude to have when you're trying to create a neighborhood hangout. Besides the physical features you've created, what's also important is who goes there, what "events" happen there, and what new features or extensions those attendees might create there. Here's a list of what you should do to make that new collection of features into a bona fide neighborhood hangout:

Show up: Woody Allen famously said that 80 percent of life is showing up. Showing up at your neighborhood hangout is fundamental to its success. You need to be out there with your kids as often as possible. Every afternoon you spend on the soccer field or driving to a crosstown playdate with your kids sucks that much life out of your neighborhood. I'm not saying that you should never leave your neighborhood, but I am saying that you should be acutely aware of the benefits of merely spending time there.

Host events: Sure, the end goal is for our kids and neighbor kids to be playing every day at our neighborhood hangouts, not to have them show up only at special events. However, events can make kids and parents comfortable with the place, facilitate relations between neighbors, and create fun memories that can serve to increase the hangout's importance in your neighborhood.

Do your best to hold these events jointly with neighbors. The more families who participate, the broader the base of invitees and attendees you'll have.

Evolve and extend: Young kids grow and evolve rapidly. So do their interests. Any place in which they hang out must grow and evolve to keep up with them. If the kids who frequent your hangout are deeply involved in the place, they will have an impulse to change it in ways that keep up with their evolving interests. Your features should accommodate this impulse. I mentioned installing "customizable" features like whiteboards and wooden playhouses before. Also think about the longevity of your purchases. A dome-style climber might be used as a climber by older kids, a playhouse by those too young to climb, and as a fort or a place to hang art from the bars.

Lastly, recall my discussion of tweens' and teens' affinity for electronic media. If you can provide electronic media capabilities in your neighborhood hangout like I have, you have a built-in way to keep your neighborhood hangout interesting to these older kids. It's easy for kids to add new digital content—DVDs, digital videos, or music—that will likely increase their time spent there.

Finally, unless you're completely convinced that your kids and neighbor kids can successfully evolve and extend your neighborhood hangout by themselves, you'll need to continue adding things yourself to keep them interested. Of course, it's best if you create joint projects with your kids to do this. For instance, you might decorate or paint your playhouse with your kids. Or, you might plan a display for Halloween with them. Or, you might help them create a skateboard obstacle course in your driveway. Projects like these necessitate that you put continuing time and energy into your neighborhood hangout—but also offers an example for your kids that investing effort and imagination in it makes for a better play space for everyone. Soon, they'll be doing the same.

Ice Rinks as Winter Hangouts

Doesn't the rink at Glen Stewart Park in Toronto look like a wonderful place to hang out in the winter?

For at least one glorious month every year, when the weather is coldest, Glen Stewart Park in the Beaches neighborhood of Toronto is filled with skaters—pleasure skaters on one side, and hockey players on the other. This is a quaint residential park, surrounded on all sides by houses. It's absolutely enchanting in the winter.

"The beautiful thing about this rink is that the kids can walk to it," said Thomas Neal, a neighbor who has taken charge of maintaining the Glen Stewart Park rink for the last 11 years. "There are lots of outdoor city rinks, but most people drive there."

Neal's family is deep into organized team hockey. He coaches one of his boys' (age 14 and 8) competitive teams. His daughter (11) figure skates at an indoor rink as well. However he considers the time his kids spend at the Glen Stewart rink to be very valuable.

"When kids play pickup hockey here in the park, they learn to skate well, to handle the puck, more than they do in structured team hockey," Neal notes. "Also, kids of different ages and ability levels get to play with each other, unlike in the leagues. In general, they get into a much wider variety of situations, so they have to get creative."

John Vlahos of Montreal, who runs mybackyardicerink.com, agrees with Neal's points about hockey skills, but notes, "The biggest value is fun. It's free time for the kids. They're on a clock all the time at indoor rinks." Vlahos' three children play practically every day of the winter on a backyard rink that he builds every year.

Building and maintaining these outdoor rinks takes an awful lot of work. In fact, the Glen Stewart Park rink, which is much larger than most backyard rinks—almost as large as a regulation hockey rink—is practically a full-time job. To set it up initially, Neal works about 15 hours a day for three or four days—many iterations of flooding with water, letting the water freeze, and smoothing.

Once it's built, he or a colleague works on maintenance for a few hours late at night, early in the morning, and before kids get out of school in the afternoon. The maintenance work is very similar to what a Zamboni machine does on an indoor rink, but outdoor conditions like fallen leaves, snow, and melting make it much more time-consuming and unpredictable.

Believe it or not, last winter, Neal did almost all of this work on his own because his trusted colleague was hurt. "I'm a real estate agent, and January is a pretty slow month. Also, because I manage my own appointments, I schedule them around my work with the rink and my coaching."

"I look forward to building our backyard rink every year," says Vlahos, who starts planning in early September for a late-November build. "It's a lot of extra work, but we really enjoy it. You know, winter's very harsh here, so building a rink makes it easier to go through." A plus is that rather than staying inside, the neighbor kids congregate almost daily and the block is alive with the sounds of laughter, shouting, and good outdoor exercise.

"It is amazing how your attitude toward winter changes after you construct your backyard rink," agrees ESPN.com hockey reporter John Buccigross, who also builds a backyard rink for his kids and neighbor kids every year. "You instantly root for cold temperatures. The cold is your ally. You are not depressed by the short, dry, cold days and nights, but rejoice in them. Without question, my life is better with my backyard rink. I'm happier, more upbeat, and more attuned to nature."[8]

CHAPTER 13

Keep Kids' Lives Simple

The profound changes in children's daily lives of the past few decades described in Chapter 2 are unprecedented in human history. Meanwhile, writes developmental psychologist Gabrielle Principe, "Modern children are born with the very same brains and accompanying tendencies, abilities, and adaptations as their nomadic hunter-gatherer ancestors dating back at least 35,000 years, but perhaps as far as 250,000."[1] This disconnect between children's brains and the world in which they live today makes parts of that world "challenging and even damaging to the development of their brains, bodies, and behaviors."[2]

Researchers are only now beginning to realize the crucial value of direct, real-world interactions to healthy child development, particularly in the early years. The American Academy of Pediatrics (AAP) recently recommended that children 2 and under consume zero screen media, and it recommends that children over the age of 2 consume a total of one to two hours per day.[3] Automobile travel forces kids to sit still and not interact with the world, which developmental psychologists contend is the exact opposite of what their developing bodies and brains need. Numerous studies indicate that unsupervised play enhances academic achievement and social skills.[4] Still other studies show that the more often families eat dinner together at home, the less likely kids are to smoke, drink, do drugs, get depressed, develop eating disorders and consider suicide, and the more likely they are to do well in school, delay having sex, and eat healthy.[5]

One of our fundamental tasks as parents is to guide our children's adaptation to our modern world, in bits and pieces over time. In this chapter, I'll argue that we should keep preschoolers' lives simple—focused on direct, real-world experience. We parents should set a foundation of simple, low-tech values and behavior in the preschool years that will give our children resilience against later social pressures to conform to a cultural norm of technology saturation and scheduled lives.

The Real World as a Fundamental Value

Children need to develop real-world skills to prosper in the real world. While children are consuming electronic media, they are not paying attention to the real world around them, nor are they using their bodies to interact with it. This means a very real possibility that our kids will be more competent with mediated, virtual worlds than they are with the real world. This is where I draw the line. It's a religious tenet of mine, in a way: "THE REAL WORLD IS PRIMARY. NO OTHER ALTERNATIVE WORLD IS AS IMPORTANT IN ANY WAY."

For instance, being able to hold a 15-minute conversation with another person is far more important for my children than chatting with others online. Building a fort with cardboard boxes is far more valuable than building a "Sim City" in a video game. Playing a baseball game is far more valuable than watching one on TV.

The list could go on for a while. Practically any real, authentic experience—an experience in the real, physical world—is always better for our children than its virtual substitute.

Children whose parents constantly hover over them in the real world by protecting them from danger are only slightly better off. Although they're not immersed in a virtual world, the version of real world they're exposed to is insulated and distorted.

You might say, "Not my child. He isn't one of those antisocial nerds." Well, does your child need a DVD or a video game or a computer to be content inside your house if you're not entertaining him or her? Can she find fun outside in your neighborhood or in the woods without the help of an adult? Can he independently negotiate and make compromises with peers? For many, if not most American parents, the answers to these questions would be "no."

I want my children to have a solid grounding in real-world skills like these from the beginning. We have a small window of opportunity with our young children to ground them in the real world and to help them develop vital real-world skills. Once they get immersed in peer culture in the tween and teen years, their ability to deeply and independently perceive the real world and learn from it diminishes markedly.

Reading this, you might guess that I'm a Luddite, an enemy of technology. Actually, I'm a career software and Internet entrepreneur and a gadget freak. I'm crazy about my Mac Book Air, iPhone, and iPad, and I use them for many hours each day.

However, I also have long face-to-face conversations every day. I know that, if I were forced to choose between face-to-face conversations and e-mail + texting every day, I'd choose the real world every time. I want my kids to do the same.

Neighborhood as a Fundamental Value

Perhaps the most important way parents can impart values to their children is through how and where they spend their time with them. Preschoolers who don't spend time with their parents in their neighborhoods will not grow up valuing their neighborhood. If parents keep their kids inside or drive around to activities every day, they're sending the message to their children that their neighborhoods—or even their own backyards—are not important.

Preschoolers' neighborhoods can easily become their most familiar place if they have help and encouragement from their parents. Because it practically takes zero time to get there, parents can, with very little effort, wander through with their children at least a bit every day. With each little bit of wandering in a familiar place, children become more comfortable and confident.

As I discussed, when these preschoolers grow up a bit and start to be independent, they will seek a hangout where they can frequently interact with the peers they care about. If they don't have a hangout in their neighborhood, most kids will spend a great deal of time hanging out on online social networks. This is true even for those kids whose parents kept them away from screens in their early years, because the drive to connect socially becomes extremely powerful.

Neighborhoods are the best place where preschool and elementary school-aged children, playing independently, can acquire valuable skills like social skills, time management, problem solving, geographical navigation, and more. These skills are building blocks toward self-reliance, a concept that I discuss in further detail in Chapter 15. What's best is that children can develop all these skills in a place that is familiar and comfortable to parents, so that those parents can remain present in and relevant to their lives.

Now that I've discussed the importance of fundamental values of the real world and the neighborhood, I'll recommend some "don'ts" and "dos" for parents.

Don't Permit Excessive Screen Time

We adults may get a great deal of enjoyment from electronic media like television, movies, or the Internet, but, as mentioned before, child development experts advocate that parents severely limit children's consumption of media. If at all possible, I recommend that parents follow the AAP recommendations of zero television for children under 2, and one to two hours per day maximum for older children.

The AAP and other critics have offered the following reasons to object to excessive electronic media consumption in children's lives:

1) It causes children to be sedentary, thus leading to obesity.

2) It causes permanent neurological changes in the brain that result in lack of attention and inability to engage in deep, complex thinking.[6]

3) Specific content such as violence or sexual content is inappropriate for children.

4) Time allocated to media crowds out time that could be allocated to more desirable activities like homework, free play, or family dinners.

The latter point is the most important, according to neurologist David Perlmutter, author of *Raise a Smarter Child by Kindergarten*. "First and foremost," he writes, "the most important issue with reference to children watching television is that the passive act of watching television displaces other activities in which the child could have been participating."[7]

Implementing a policy restricting screen time will be different for each family, but I'll say here that it's easier for kids to go without television and other digital media if they don't see their parents consuming it. In that case, they have no idea what they're missing. Thus, a family that has no television around to attract children's eyes, at least when they're present, solves this problem. This is what my wife, Perla, and I did until recently. Our kids hardly ever saw screens flashing images, so they didn't crave it for themselves.

The exceptions were when we went to other people's homes, or the many brief instances when my wife or I glanced at our iPhones or our laptops in front of our boys. The latter often caused anxiety in our boys, which continues today. In her book *Alone Together*, Sherry Turkle describes her broad findings on this problem: "Over and over, kids raised the same three examples of feeling hurt and not wanting to show it when their mom or dad would be on their devices instead of paying attention to them: at meals, during pickup after either school or an extracurricular activity, and during sports events."[8]

It's quite difficult to totally shut our kids off from digital media. Like it or not, at some point, every family needs to manage how to incorporate digital media into kids' lives in a positive way. I'll discuss how Perla and I have done this for television in the section "Do Manage Television Time."

Don't Drive When You Can Walk or Bike

Automobile travel is a dominant factor in most children's lives. They spend, on average, about 45 minutes per day as passengers of automobiles.[9] Those are by far the most dangerous 45 minutes of a child's day. The No. 1 cause of death among children in America is motor vehicle accidents in which they are passengers.[10] However, this is but one of many reasons to walk or bike your kids, rather than drive them.

Fundamentally, driving leads to a focused, clock-driven, adult-controlled lifestyle, whereas walking and biking leads to an exploring, serendipitous, child-controlled lifestyle. Preschoolers are at their happiest and learn the most when they are exploring on their own, moving their bodies, but they cannot explore when they are strapped into a car seat, watching the backs of our heads. Remember that only adults are allowed to drive, so only they have the feeling of being free and in control when they drive their children in a car. Conversely, when adults and children walk together, they are equals, and toddlers, in particular, accentuate this point by wandering off on their own incessantly.

Once children arrive at a destination by car, parents usually continue to limit their freedom because the place is not very familiar, and is populated with many strangers. In other words, children remain under the close supervision of adults. They're better off when they can explore on their own in familiar territory.

When making a decision on how to get to a particular place, such as school or the store, strongly consider walking children in a stroller or riding bikes rather than driving. Although it can be tempting to get places faster in a car, when time allows, enjoy the richer, slower experience, perhaps stopping to play with someone or something along the way.

Elementary school children can walk or bike to school under their own power, and in many neighborhoods, may eventually go on their own without being accom-

Since he started kindergarten, Marco has ridden to and from his elementary school, a 1 1/2 mile ride, every day, rain or shine. All that first year, an adult accompanied him both ways. Starting in first grade, he began to make these trips on his own. Doing this has been tremendously valuable for him in many ways.

panied by an adult. In 1969, approximately half of all elementary and intermediate schoolchildren walked or biked to school independently. Today, that figure for children of ages 5 to 15 is less than 15 percent.[11] Parents usually overestimate the dangers of walking or biking to school and underestimate the benefits. At the very least, I suggest that parents make an honest effort to have their children walk or bike, with or without their help, at the beginning of the school year.

In addition, parents should pare down their children's activities and leave more time for neighborhood walking and biking, where children have more opportunity to build independent life skills and feel more in control and autonomous. These trips are less about efficiency and more about finding serendipity. Children are almost certain to make unexpected stops, detours, and discoveries because they can.

Do Let Children Play on Their Own

This sounds so simple, but many parents these days have a hard time leaving their children alone when they play with each other. Instead, they hover. A lot. They hover to make sure their kids aren't in danger. They hover to exploit learning opportunities. They hover to ensure smooth social relations between their children and other children. They hover to make sure that kids are playing games the "right way."

Unfortunately, when children are being followed so closely by their parents, they don't play like they do without them around. In fact, some child development experts would argue that, when supervised closely by parents, children don't play at all, and they don't have nearly as much fun. Plus, they don't learn as much. Anthony Pellegrini finds that children's play and speaking are more sophisticated when adults aren't around.[12] Another study by Roger Mackett finds that when children are outdoors without adults, they take more time to explore and go off the beaten path.[13] In other words, they're less efficient at getting from point A to point B, but they learn more.

Parents can play a constructive role if they're in the general area where children are playing, but that role is more of facilitator than controller. When kids get hungry or thirsty, parents can provide food or drink. When kids get hurt, parents can provide a Band-Aid and a hug. When kids get into a physical fight, parents can mediate. When kids need some item for their play, parents can provide it. Other than doing things like this, parents should stay out of the way, letting kids choose what they play and how, and parents should even let kids work out nonviolent squabbles by themselves.

Do Manage Television Time

Most parents tightly control children's play, but let their kids do whatever they want, for as long as they want, in front of screens—televisions, video game consoles, and computers. I think this is totally backward. Play should be fairly free, but television time in the preschool and early elementary school years should be tightly controlled.

Perla and I recently started introducing television to our older kids—Marco (7) and Nico (4). We came to the conclusion that there's just too much quality programming to continue our total ban. Still, their total watching time is never more than an hour a day, and often, it's zero. Here's how we control their viewing experience to maximize the benefits:

Make TV a family activity: Our TV only gets turned on when Perla or I can watch with our kids. We watch TV together in our family room much like we eat dinner together in our dining room. This enables us to control the experience and interact with our kids about what we're watching.

Control the remote: Because I control the remote, our kids never see anything that I don't approve of. Once I allow them to see something, they know about it and may ask for it again, or they may ask for something related. That's fine by me.

No live TV: With DVDs, streaming video programming, and YouTube videos, as opposed to live TV, I can choose exactly what my boys watch and when, and we can totally avoid commercials. Furthermore, I can (and do) stop video from these sources very frequently to explain things. This enables me to show them programming that's aimed at higher age groups. For instance, they loved watching the adult-oriented movie *Apollo 13* only because I stopped it frequently to discuss or clarify.

Furthermore, research suggests that they learn an awful lot more because they were interacting with a real person—me—and not just passively watching a screen. Patricia Kuhl and her colleagues exposed two different groups of babies to a native Mandarin speaker in person and on TV over a four-week period. The babies who interacted with the Mandarin speaker in person were able to recognize Mandarin sounds, but the babies who watched the same speaker on TV were not. From this and other studies, researchers conclude that young children learn far more from live humans than from images of humans on TV. So, one might view my TV sessions with my kids as the TV content setting up the real "teachable moments" for me in person.

Use real-world interests to drive content choices: We let our boys' interests in the real world drive what we choose for them to watch. In the recent past, the subject areas we've focused on are geology, the solar system and space travel, parkour (videos in which people—usually young men—jump and tumble from building to building), and, of course, children's neighborhood lives (kids jumping on trampolines or building forts). Believe me, between vast online video libraries like YouTube and all the available DVDs out there, it's easy to find lots and lots of great video content relevant to any possible interest area. If we have no video content relevant to any real-world interests today, we watch no TV. TV is not a time filler.

Recall that Dr. Perlmutter claims that TV time displaces time spent on other, more developmentally valuable activities. However, I've guided my boys' TV watching in a way that actually enhances their non-TV lives. In other words, their intellectual, social, and physical development away from the TV is more advanced than it would be if they were not watching TV. The videos we watch in geology and the solar system increase their knowledge of science and math. The videos we watch in parkour inspire them to collaborate on their own daredevil tricks, increasing their physical agility and social skills. The programs we watch about children's neighborhood lives teach them lessons they can apply every day when they're in our neighborhood.

In the meantime, I haven't heard a word from my boys about mindless live TV programs like SpongeBob or the like, nor have I heard any complaints that they don't get to watch on their own. They are caught up in a virtuous circle because their real-world activities help them understand the videos they watch, and vice versa. Far from subtracting from their real-world activities, the TV they watch breathes life into them.

Do Have Family Dinners Every Night

As mentioned previously, studies show that the more often families eat dinner together at home, the less likely kids are to smoke, drink, do drugs, get depressed, develop eating disorders, and consider suicide, and the more likely they are to do well in school, delay having sex, and eat healthy.[14]

Wow. It's no wonder that experts claim that there is nothing more important in family life than having family dinners at home. For our purposes here, I'll add another benefit of having family dinners every night: They give parents and children more opportunity to spend time in their neighborhood. I play outside with my boys after dinner every night during daylight savings time, and even when it's dark after dinner, we dabble in night games like flashlight tag.

I recommend that families do whatever it takes to have family dinners together at home as many nights as possible. That means that parents should try to avoid work commitments that overlap with dinnertime, and they also should avoid committing their children to activities that do the same. Structured activities, especially sports teams, often routinely schedule things like practices during dinnertime. Before signing up for any high-commitment activity, you should weigh the benefit against the cost of diminished family dinners. Perla and I intend to totally avoid activities that would jeopardize dinnertime.

Do Expose Them to Stories of Children in Neighborhoods

Where can our children turn for role models of how to live a life of free play in their neighborhood? After all, they're unlikely to know any kids who do so, and contemporary media don't portray kids who play outside, either. The only possible role models come from stories of children's lives from decades ago, the so-called "Golden Age of Childhood," when free outdoor play was commonplace.

Everyone loves stories, children in particular. Fundamentally, a good story grips them emotionally, holds their attention, and lingers in their memories. Certainly, it often teaches a moral lesson, but it entertains first, and teaches second.

Oral Storytelling

First and foremost, parents should opt for the oldest and most low-tech method for transmitting stories—oral storytelling. In the days before electronic media, stories told by family members at the dinner table were the entertainment for the evening. In Ireland, dinners at the family hearth were often formal affairs for storytelling, where itinerant storytellers would regularly come to tell a story in exchange for a meal and a night of lodging.[15] These stories were often two hours long or more—the equivalent of a family movie today.

Most parents have a wealth of neighborhood stories from their childhood. My kids ask me to tell them one every night when they go to bed. Every night. That's more than 2,000 story sessions over their childhoods so far! Fortunately for me, they let me repeat stories sometimes.

When telling a story, offer protagonists who are relatable and have faults.[16] In my father's stories of his childhood in 1930s and '40s Pittsburgh, he comes across as both sympathetic and flawed. For instance, he would sneak into places with his friends rather than pay the entry fee because his family was poor; and he was insecure with girls, partly because of the appearance of his nose—he broke it three times and it got bigger each time. You also need conflict and, ideally, an adventure that includes unstructured experiences with peers—further reinforcing that being outside and unsupervised equals a good time, even if it's not always easy.

The main reason my father's stories about his shack in the alley behind his house are so memorable for me is that building it and maintaining it was such a struggle. Dad and his friends scrounged for materials from all over to build it, and they locked it up to keep other kids from trying to use it or steal things from it. Then, one day in the winter, the potbellied stove they put in there to keep it warm caused a fire, and it burned to the ground. After the initial shock of seeing their hangout destroyed, they built it again—even better. This is a much more entertaining story than if they had gotten wood from their parents, built a shack with ease, and had uninterrupted good times there. And certainly, Dad's tales inspired me to build tree shacks and forts with my friends.

Children's Books

Reading books to children is another low-tech way to expose children to stories about children and neighborhoods. Here, I'll describe a few of my favorites on this subject that I've read to my children over and over.

The Big Orange Splot, by children's author and NPR commentator Daniel Pinkwater, tells the tale of a man named Mr. Plumbean who lives on a "neat street"—a street where all houses look exactly the same. One day, Mr. Plumbean decides to radically personalize the look of the front of his home, destroying the neat street's uniformity, and he becomes the only person on his neighborhood to hang out in his front yard and entertain guests there. One by one, neighbors come by to try to convince him to change his house back to conform with the others, but instead, they end up personalizing the fronts of their homes, too. The neat street is destroyed, but everyone enjoys being in their neighborhood a lot more.

Roxaboxen is a true story from a neighborhood in early 20th-century Arizona. Kids there created a play town in a vacant lot out of found objects—mostly rocks and boxes. The town became a complete society, with an economy, laws, and wars. I've used *Roxaboxen* as a catalyst to get my kids to create their own play town and society in a creek bed close to my house.

The Raft[17] is a semiautobigraphical tale about a boy who spends the summer at the rural home of his grandmother. At first, the boy is resistant to staying there. "There's nobody to play with. . . . She doesn't even have a TV," he says. However, he comes to appreciate the serenity and profound appeal of life there, especially the river and his grandmother's special raft.

Weslandia[18] is the story of a boy named Wesley who's different from all the other kids he knows. He tinkers in his backyard, creating a sophisticated agriculture-based world there called "Weslandia." Slowly, he sparks interest among other kids, and eventually, they come to respect him and want to be his friend.

The Busy Life of Ernestine Buckmeister[19] is the story of a girl who's overscheduled with after-school activities, and longs for a more playful life like her next-door neighbor, Hugo. Eventually, she rebels, dragging her nanny to the park to frolic without a plan.

Television and Movies

Few TV shows and movies made today depict children playing independently in their neighborhoods, but there are many great ones made depicting children in the mid-20th century that you can get on DVD.

Perhaps the most popular television show ever that depicts children's neighborhood lives is the 1950s and 1960s show *Leave It to Beaver*. My older sons, Marco and Nico, absolutely adore the DVDs we have of the show. Beaver Cleaver has an incredibly rich neighborhood life that, by today's standards, is quite astonishing. In the first six episodes alone (there were 234 in total), in which he's 7 years old, Beaver walks to school by himself, goes on his own to get a haircut, makes friends with adults not known to his parents, and has many solo adventures outside. It's clear to me that Beaver learns far more about how to deal with the real world than practically every child today. This is ironic considering the common conception of Beaver's childhood as being overly sheltered.

Mister Rogers' Neighborhood is a great TV show about neighborhood life for preschool kids. Rogers plays himself, wandering through a miniature neighborhood, striking up conversations with regular puppet characters and discussing life lessons.

Fat Albert and the Cosby Kids was based on Bill Cosby's remembrances of his childhood in a low-income neighborhood of Philadelphia in the 1940s and 1950s. Cosby's voice is behind many of the animated characters, including Fat Albert and his famous and hearty "Hey, hey, hey!"

A great show for depicting adolescent life in the neighborhood is *The Wonder Years*, set in the 1960s. Kevin Arnold, his best friend Paul, and his puppy love interest, Winnie Cooper, are close neighbors. They appear in many memorable scenes, including the pilot episode in which Kevin and Winnie share their first kiss in the woods in their neighborhood. In a later episode, those woods were bulldozed to make room for a new shopping mall. Unfortunately, no official DVD set was ever made of this show due to music rights problems, but "pirate" DVDs of *The Wonder Years* are widely available—just search for "the wonder years dvd" on the Web.

My favorite film about childhood, *Stand by Me*, is a wonderful coming-of-age story about four 12-year-old neighbor boys set in 1959. They tell their parents they're having a sleepover with each other, but instead, they embark on a memorable overnight adventure to find the body of a local boy who died recently.

Photo: "UNTITLED XI Nevada 2010", by Christoph Gielen

CHAPTER 14

Make a Village

When my father speaks of his "old neighborhood," he's thinking about a few blocks in Pittsburgh's Hill District decades ago, where groups of neighbor families chatted every summer evening on their front stoops, and where children played in the sidewalk in front of his house and in the alley behind. He knew everyone there – dozens of children and adults – very well, and they knew him well, too. Thus, he was comfortable there, and he was safe. His parents didn't worry about him because he was in an environment that was very familiar to him and to them.

Unfortunately for children today, neighbors hardly know each other these days. In fact, the quaint term "village," as it's used in the old African proverb "It takes a village to raise a child," is in danger. In the introduction of her book *It Takes a Village*,[1] Hillary Clinton claims that the original notion of a village is quaint and outdated. She writes, "The village can no longer be defined as a place on the map." Instead, "it is the network of values and relationships that support and affect our lives." Even 50 years ago, communications theorist Marshall McLuhan coined the term "global village" to argue that mass communications technology had created a single, global culture.

The problem with this modern village concept for young children is that they can't use the technologies that adults routinely use to go beyond a small geographic area on their own. They can't drive cars on their own until they reach the age of 16, and they can't interact with others using technologies like mobile phones or texting until sometime in the elementary or middle school years.

So, the vast majority of young children have no village of their own. They have no place where they can feel comfortable and safe, while not under the gaze of their parents.

I strongly believe that it takes a village—an old-fashioned, tight-knit neighborhood—to raise a child. Not some "network of values and relationships." Not a "global village." In this chapter, I explore what it means to make a real, old-fashioned village for kids out of your neighborhood, and how to make that happen.

What Is a Child's Village?

It's interesting to think about what a child's village is. After all, a village is only relevant to a child if he personally has his own close relationships with neighbors, and those relationships affect his life. To take that one step further, I define a child's own village as the area within which he is comfortable roaming unsupervised. Places where his parents take him, but where he's forbidden to go on his own, are part of his parents' village, but not his. Within the boundaries of a child's village, he is intimately familiar with numerous people and physical features.

To the right is a map of the village of my oldest son, Marco, in spring 2011, when he was almost 7. Its boundaries are defined by houses of families he knows well (I changed the names) and our creek on the far right. In that area to the right of our house, he doesn't know that many people well, but they see each other a lot because he walks down our street to go to the creek often.

When I drew a map of Marco's village a year before I drew this one, it was just a few houses to either side of us on our street, and it did not include any streets because Marco had yet to venture on streets on his own. In spring 2011, he rode his bike on or walked along streets often. Two years from now, I expect that Marco's village will extend over a far greater area.

If children remain limited to their yards until the age in which they start spending lots of time on mobile phones and computers, their "village" comes to be defined as Hillary Clinton and Marshall McLuhan defined it. In other words, their village is in the virtual world, and they never establish a real-world, old-fashioned village. That's the case for most children today.

It Takes a Kid's Village to Make a Playborhood

Marco's village has lots of people he knows and cares about, lots of things for him to do, and many of what urban planning pioneer Jane Jacobs called "eyes on the street" to watch out for him. This is what it takes to make a Playborhood.

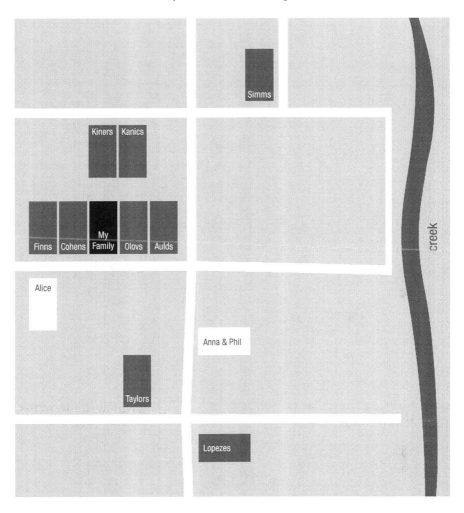

Kids are the most important people to him in his village. Families with kids are indicated by the gray houses in the map above. However, adults are very important, too, especially the parents of friends. In addition, the two neighbors who don't have kids, indicated by white houses, know Marco pretty well and serve as eyes on the street for him.

It's important for all members of the neighborhood to be connected, not just the kids. In other words, adults should have close relationships with each other, and also kids should have close relationships with adults, especially other kids' parents. The neighborhood should be a total village, not solely a kids' village. A recent study confirms this. It finds that children play more in neighborhoods where mothers think their neighbors are likely to help children and other adults.[2]

Why is this true? Children, even the most independent among them, need support from adults. They need to eat food throughout the day, and parents or babysitters usually provide that. When they get hurt, they often need an adult to comfort them or fix up a wound. When two children fight, an adult often needs to intervene. Or, the kids may be working on a project that calls for items not readily available. A parent might be called on to find a hammer in a toolbox, or to drive the kids to the office supply store to buy posters and markers.

When these needs arise, it's most convenient for a child to get help from which-ever adult is close by. The need may go unmet if the child has to run back home, a block away. So, the child must feel comfortable getting parent-like care from a friend's parent, and vice versa, the parent must step up to provide that care for the child. In order for parents to feel comfortable letting their children play in the neighborhood, or at other kids' homes, they must feel comfortable with the parents of other children.

Certainly, there are examples from neighborhoods of the past where only the kids had close relationships, and adults didn't have relationships with neighborhood kids and didn't know each other well. For instance, my father's parents were Ital-ian immigrants who never learned to speak English, so they were not able to forge close relationships with English-speaking neighbors. However, in today's world, when parents are so much more protective than they used to be, these additional relationships have become essential.

Sociologist William Julius Wilson coined the term "reciprocal guardian behavior" to describe the phenomenon of adults caring for children in urban poor neighbor-hoods. There, the principal responsibility of adults is ensuring all children's safety. Lyman Place is an excellent illustration of an urban poor neighborhood where reciprocal guardian behavior has improved children's lives. I believe, however, that the benefits of this approach extend to all social classes. Palo Alto is one of the most affluent towns in America, but recall that Jennifer Antonow of Camp Iris Way is creating a "neighborhood bill of rights." Essentially, this idea is to get parents there to agree to a set of reciprocal guardian behaviors such as making lunch for all kids present at one's house at lunchtime. These are the kinds of agreements that can easily be forged between neighbors on the same block.

N Street is perhaps the best example of reciprocal guardian behavior, as evidenced by Lucy's story and the coming-of-age ceremony. All children there benefit greatly from having many high-quality relationships with adults.

These examples show how simple steps taken by neighbors can begin the process of making a village that will be beneficial to all.

Barriers to Making a Village

Automobile Traffic

In Chapter 11, I presented the results of a study that shows how traffic on a street destroys neighbor relations. Unfortunately, making cars slow down is extremely difficult. If you live on a very busy street with lights and a constant stream of cars, but you really want to live in a village-like setting so you kids can grow up in a Playborhood, you may need to consider moving.

If your street has occasional cars, but more than you'd like, there are two things that you can do to diminish traffic there. The quick-and-simple thing you can do is put a "Children Playing" sign in the middle of your street and play with your kids there often.[3] I do this. The short-term effect of this strategy is to significantly slow down traffic. The long-term effect is to get some drivers to avoid your street and try to use another route.

The more long-term solution would be to try to get your town or city to install some sort of traffic calming feature on your street. This could be a circle or bollards at a nearby intersection or speed bumps along the road. This option should be considered only if you know that your local government is prepared and willing to act on traffic calming requests. Otherwise, you'll probably be fighting a very long and difficult battle.

Fear of Crime

Certainly, in neighborhoods that have high crime rates, neighbor relations suffer because residents stay inside, fearful of being victims of crime. Whether crime rates are in fact high or not, the fear of crime causes fewer people to go outside, which invites more crime. Neighborhoods with few people outside lack eyes on the street.

It's interesting to note that many suburban neighborhoods that start out very safe also have few eyes on the street. The worst of these are gated communities and extremely affluent neighborhoods, in which every multimillion-dollar home is surrounded by high fences. Presumably, these high barriers are meant to keep out crime, but their primary practical impact is to make their streets very inhospitable to pedestrians.

Probably the best way to combat this perception of crime, deserved or not, is to somehow get more eyes on the street. The most fundamental thing parents can do to start getting more eyes on the street is to get out there often and socialize with any neighbors they see. That can help those neighbors feel more comfortable spending time on the block, and before long, it may start to feel like a friendly village.

Suburban Sprawl

Fear of crime isn't the only reason that most suburban neighborhoods have next to no neighborhood life. The suburban model of development, built around the automobile, is perhaps an even bigger culprit: Homogeneous communities of hundreds of houses are built with few, if any walkable destinations. If inhabitants want to go to a retail store or park or school, they usually need to drive there, either because they're too far away or because walking there necessitates crossing a large street. The roads that connect these communities to destinations and to each other are wide roads with high speed limits, built to move large numbers of cars efficiently. The designs of the fronts of homes with huge, prominent garages and no porches in front emphasize cars over community.

Lastly, the fact that suburban parents' jobs are often far away from the neighborhoods they live in has two negative consequences for their neighborhood relations. First, they must spend a great deal of time commuting to and from work every day. Second, and perhaps more importantly, few, if any, of the friends and acquaintances they have at work live in their neighborhood.

So, much like the case of crime-ridden inner-city neighborhoods, residents of these suburban neighborhoods don't spend time outside, destroying any possibility for a village atmosphere. Parents have few opportunities to get to know one another, so reciprocal guardian behavior rarely happens.

Ideas for Making a Village

Below are some ideas for enhancing neighbor relations between parents, and between parents and kids. If you do some of these well, perhaps you can transform your neighborhood into an old-fashioned, friendly village.

With so many homes packed together, inhabitants of these large suburban tracts are forced to get into their cars to do just about anything. Photo: Christolph Gielen

Organize Regular Neighborhood Free Play Days

Kids' lives are so scheduled these days that parents in many neighborhoods have carved out time every week for their kids to play together. In his book *Parenting Without Fear*, Paul Donahue writes about how he, his wife, and other neighborhood parents in their suburban Westchester County, N.Y., town run an event called "Hangout Fridays."[4] Every Friday, parents bring their kids to one of the families' houses, and the kids gather together to play outside (weather permitting) while the parents sit and socialize among themselves. A friend of mine in Palo Alto participates in something very similar with neighbors every Thursday afternoon at a local park.

Because there are around a dozen children at Hangout Fridays, and because they range in age from 5 to 13, these events have less pressure and structure than a typical one-on-one playdate between two children of identical ages. These gatherings have resulted in more independent play on weekends, when the older children often get together on their own, because of the friendships that are created there.

How do you implement a neighborhood free play day in practice? It should start with a core of a few families of similar ages that are committed to it. It's best if you can settle on one regular location, either one family's yard or a nearby park. That way, kids and their parents or nannies will look for kids there regardless of any communications that week. As for communications, it's a good idea to send out an e-mail to a list every week just to tell people the play day is going to happen, even if it becomes a solid, regular event.

Tear Down Fences

With this and the following recommendation, Kevin Wolf and his colleagues started what became the N Street Cohousing Community. Tearing down even one fence between neighbors is a powerful statement. As was mentioned previously, if neighbors carefully dismantle and store the fence boards, they can feel reassured that they can simply assemble the fence again if they feel they need to do so.

Meanwhile, with their fence torn down, neighbors can enjoy a more open, expansive feeling in their backyard, as well as a more communal living experience.

Dump Your Kids on a Neighborhood Family—And Return the Favor

Families with children of similar ages can help each other out and get to know each other better by making an informal agreement to trade off taking care of each other's kids. For instance, two parent couples might trade one dinnertime a week so that each couple can have a "date night."

Or, families can simply let each other know that they can pinch-hit for each other if need be. This can start with a small childcare favor on a weekend day when, for instance, a mom wants to run to the supermarket quickly and doesn't want the hassle of taking her kids there. It just might be easier to drop the kids off at a neighbor's for a half hour. Once one family does this, it feels compelled to return the favor, and the kids start getting used to it.

If this becomes a regular habit, the kids will get to know each other a lot better, and parents' lives will improve, too, with the added flexibility.

Plant a Community Garden

A community garden—a garden that is openly accessible to all neighbors—greatly enhances neighbor relations. In addition, they can be a great learning laboratory for children. Different community gardens have different rules, but in general, they encourage cooperation between participants. Even in gardens where different neighbors have their own plots, many resources such as tools and fertilizer are shared. Also, when neighbors are working the garden at the same time, they have an opportunity to get to know each other better.

There are three models of a community garden. The traditional model is where the government of a city like New York or San Francisco has converted many unused patches of public land into community gardens. According to the American Community Gardening Association, there are about 18,000 official community gardens in the United States.

However, even this large number isn't enough to reach where most people live. These people have two options. One is to simply cultivate public or semipublic space that is not being used. An example of such land might be a vacant lot or an odd public strip of land such as a traffic circle, median, or a strip between the sidewalk and the street.

The other option, for those who have a front yard, is to create a plot there with open access for neighbors. This is most commonly done to encourage participation by children. One outstanding example of this is Karen Harwell's Dana Meadows Organic Children's Garden in Palo Alto. She's devoted her entire yard—about 5,000 square feet—to this garden. In that space, she's crammed 17 different fruit trees, numerous vegetables, ducks, and beehives. The yard also contains many facilities that make the garden sustainable, like a compost pile and worm pile. Harwell actively invites neighborhood children to participate in her garden with her, and, as a teacher who studied biology in college, she uses that opportunity to teach them many important biological principles.

You can also do this on a much smaller scale. Consider devoting a parking strip or bit of your front yard to a small vegetable patch or flower garden with markers to indicate what's growing there. You can invite neighbor children to help you plan and prep this space, or just welcome them to explore it when they happen by. Soon, your house will become a place where children feel safe congregating, exploring, and meeting one another.

Have Regular Community Dinners

Simply eating at a neighbor's house one time is a simple but powerful step in community building that few people ever take. If you do it once and it feels good, you should ask your neighbors to trade off cooking and hosting a dinner periodically, perhaps once every week or two. Kevin Wolf of N Street recommends that each host make the meal rather than having a potluck each time, because the total amount of work is reduced that way. Making one bigger meal every three or four times is easier than making something to share every time.

Ultimately, once you coordinate schedules and learn each others' food preferences, you'll save time and have fun sharing a bit of each other's lives. Naturally, the kids will play while the parents visit, and they'll enjoy exploring and becoming comfortable in someone else's home. If weekly dinners with neighbors seems a bit daunting, start by hosting one initial dinner with neighbors where you can talk about making it a regular event. Who knows—you may eventually enjoy this so much that you decide to do it even more than once a week.

Run a Neighborhood Summer Camp

Jennifer Antonow and Diana Nemet's idea behind running Camp Iris Way is to introduce to parents and kids the idea that they can stay in their neighborhoods and have fun all summer, not for just that week. Their hope is that, by attending a fun neighborhood summer camp, kids will get more comfortable with each other and with the place after the camp is over.

In fact, they have made great strides toward this goal, and they have also enhanced relations between parents and between parents and kids in other families. I have also accomplished this, albeit to a lesser degree, at Camp Yale.

Organize Block Parties

Another one-time event that can result in lots of neighborhood bonding is a block party. These can be amazingly fun events, but organizing them can be very time-consuming, too. It might seem a bit foolish to spend days organizing an event that lasts one afternoon when our priority should be on getting our kids outside playing every day. However, block parties can be uniquely valuable because they get practically everyone in the neighborhood out and talking to one another, not just the neighbors who are friends. They're an opportunity for you and your kids to talk to and play with neighbors outside of your close circle of friends. At best, block parties might result in new friendships, but even at worst, you and your kids can maintain some contact with neighbors you hardly ever see.

In Seattle, block parties are a citywide affair on a certain summer evening that is scheduled by the city. Each neighborhood is encouraged to participate with someone acting as block leader to organize the potluck and such, but the city provides street closure signs and flyers. The police department sponsors it because knowing your neighbors equals decreased crime. Of course, some blocks create a more elaborate party (see Chapter 9, "Dibble Avenue: Seattle") and some do the bare minimum, but either way, all neighborhoods gain a lot from having one.

Hold Family Social Events with Neighbors

Now that you have children, you sometimes plan family outings with families that have children of similar ages to yours. You may not be very good friends with the adults in those families, but your own enjoyment is no longer the singular objective of your social life. It's often more important that the children get along well.

I recommend making an extra effort to hold these kinds of social events with families from our neighborhoods, because doing so will improve our children's everyday life. If your family participates in a Saturday outing with another family that lives 15 minutes away by car, you're strengthening relationships between children that will require a car ride by a parent every time to maintain. On the other hand, if you have the same outing with a neighborhood family, you're making it more likely that your kids will get together spontaneously anytime they have free time, with no need for parents' intervention. The same goes for inviting the neighbors—even if they're not your kids' closest friends—to events like birthday parties, egg hunts, holiday gift exchanges, or other seasonal family fun.

Make a Neighborhood Hangout

Having your kids and neighbor kids spend time outside is crucial for them to develop attachment to their neighborhood. Nothing is more important for kids to spend time outside regularly than having a hangout, so if there is no obvious hangout close to your house, you or your neighbors will need to make one in one or more of your yards, or a public space nearby.

Walk and Bike in the Neighborhood

Every time you zoom through your neighborhood in your car with your children, you're devaluing all the places and people you pass by. Alternatively, when you walk or bike in your neighborhood, you and your children are much more likely to experience the sights and sounds there, and to appreciate it more. This is true whether you're going to a particular destination or just taking an evening stroll.

Play with Your Kids in Your Yard or on the Street

In Chapter 3, I discussed the "Neighborhood Play Evangelism" my kids and I practice in our neighborhood. This is vital for creating a village for kids, especially for those too young to roam around on their own. If you want to generate more activity for your kids, you need them to be playing visibly—out front—at every opportunity. If you have little or no yard space, have them play on the sidewalk, or start parking somewhere other than the driveway so you can use that.

Knock on Neighbors' Doors

When my boys and I don't see anyone outside, we often go to the houses of neighbor kids and knock on their doors. If you want a Playborhood culture, you've got to encourage it by creating a culture of spontaneous drop-bys and invitations to play. Once you get the ball rolling, others will follow suit.

Celebrate Birthdays in Your Home or Yard

More and more parents are throwing children's birthday parties at a jumpy house, a kids' gym, a fun restaurant, or a public park miles away from their homes. What's wrong with our homes? Our yards? Our neighborhoods?

Does it matter that we're passing the most significant moments of our lives at places we don't care about? Places we have no emotional connection to? I believe it does. Big time.

Every time we hold a birthday party at our home or yard, we leave some memories there. We keep adding things or changing things to make our homes a great place to entertain. Memorable things happen at specific places in our yard. The kids might play a particularly fun game of hide-and-seek among the bushes across the front yards. We might decorate the fort and have the party take place almost entirely in there. One year, all the kids wrote happy birthday messages on the dry-erase board on our fence. We take photographs that capture these moments, as well as how our homes looked at that particular time.

Of course, it's entirely possible for us to do all these things at various other venues, but then these venues would be mere settings, mere backdrops. However, if we hold these events at our home or yard, these memories accumulate over time to form a rich tapestry.

In the three years since moving into our house, my wife and I have thrown every birthday party right here. I can honestly say these have been the best birthday parties I've ever attended. Ever. Parents and kids have an equally amazing time. Often, these are more affordable than a "destination party," and though it may seem like more work to have it at home, it gets easier—and more fun—every year you do it.

Make Halloween a Big Neighborhood Event

Halloween can be a very special bonding event for your neighborhood because practically all families participate, and because the costumes and decorations make for a uniquely festive atmosphere. For many Playborhoods like mine, it's the most important day of the year.

If your neighborhood has any sort of Halloween spirit at all, you should make it a big event for your kids. Put special attention and time into preparation: decorating the outside of your house and shopping for or making kids' costumes. Then, on Halloween evening, participate to the fullest: Hand out treats at home, and take your kids to every nearby home for trick or treat (or, if they're old enough, send them out on their own). Talk with lots of kids and adults. In my neighborhood on Halloween, we have hundreds of trick-or-treaters. I make meaningful contact with as many kids and parents on that one evening than I do in the rest of the year.

Simon Firth of Palo Alto does something extra every year that pulls his kids together with their neighborhood friends: He and his wife host an early Halloween potluck dinner for kids in costume. From there, they start right into trick or treating in large groups, together. Samantha Stack of Seattle organized a "mischief night" on her block for the night before Halloween, where neighbor kids went to each participating house for a different simple activity, including a scavenger hunt, a freeze dancing contest, arts and crafts, and a mummy wrapping game with rolls of toilet paper. Each house hosted for about 30 minutes with very little prep or expense, and the kids loved it.

I strongly recommend that you do not drive your kids to another neighborhood for Halloween. You should not view Halloween as merely a night of entertainment. It's the biggest opportunity of the year to strengthen the "village" quality of your neighborhood.

Ask Your Nannies or Babysitters to Stay in the Neighborhood

Most of us who leave our kids at home with nannies or babysitters during the workday don't specifically ask those nannies to spend time in our neighborhoods. This is a mistake. Nannies or babysitters aren't "invested" in our neighborhoods like we are because they don't live there. Many would rather take our kids to a park blocks or miles away to meet up with a friend than stay close to home. This may pass the time for our kids, but it doesn't help them build neighborhood relationships.

If we want them to participate in this goal with us, we have to give them explicit instructions to do so. We need to tell them to play in the front yard with our kids rather than take them to a park, and we need to explain which neighbors' doors to knock on. Make it a point to introduce your caregiver to all your neighbors, and be sure he or she feels comfortable calling or visiting key houses so that your kids' play isn't solitary when you're not around.

CHAPTER 15

Encourage Self-Reliance

Twentysomethings in America are in trouble. They are less likely than those of a generation ago to hold a steady career-track job, to live away from their parents, to be financially independent, or to be in a committed relationship.[1] Moreover, they're unprepared to make moral judgments like why one shouldn't drink and drive, have indiscriminate sex, practice materialism, or ignore the needs of others in civic society.[2]

As a result, there's a movement in psychology to define a new life stage between adolescence and adulthood called "emerging adulthood." The idea, to put it simply, is that these people emerging from adolescence aren't ready for adulthood, so they need to spend 10 years or so getting their act together before they can be adults. They are independent, but not stable; able to work, but do it with one eye closed; dating, but without any thought of commitment; confronted by moral choices, but unequipped to think them through.

Those of us who grew up faster might think that passing through one's 20s with few responsibilities would be lots of fun. However, the increasing trend of depression and other emotional disorders for twentysomethings tells a very different story. As I mentioned in Chapter 1, more than 11 percent of young adults aged 18-24 in 2001–02 were found to have depressive disorders, and 95.7 percent of university psychological counseling directors believe that psychological problems have been increasing among university students in recent years.

Ironically, parents' push to make their kids grow up too fast is a big reason why those kids aren't fully ready to become adults when they reach their 20s. Rather than letting their "kids be kids" and play freely, they push their kids to excel in school and in structured activities. Thus, they make it much more difficult for their children to fully explore their inner forces that lead them to be intrinsically motivated.

In his best-selling book *Drive*,[3] Daniel Pink writes about how employers can get their adult employees to be intrinsically motivated by emphasizing three elements of intrinsic motivation: autonomy, mastery, and purpose. In *The Path to Purpose*, William Damon finds teenagers and young adults from age 12 to 22 quite lacking in purposefulness. In fact, Pink contends in *Drive* that purpose is the final, and perhaps the most elusive piece of the intrinsic motivation puzzle, the "third leg" that defines the context through which autonomy and mastery are expressed.[4]

In this chapter, I'll focus on how parents can encourage those first two legs of intrinsic motivation, autonomy and mastery, by discussing a rather old-fashioned concept: self-reliance. "Self" is roughly equivalent to autonomy, and "reliance" is tied to the concept of mastery in that one needs to master skills in order to rely on them. I'll describe the problem of deficient self-reliance skills in children and propose an approach to parenting and play that attacks this problem. In a nutshell, I recommend that we parents should facilitate our children's lives more, and control them less.

Self-Reliance as a Parenting Objective

I really felt bad for this kid I saw at a bike shop recently. He was in his late teens, quite tall, about 6'2", and he was holding his bike against his hip, but he didn't say a word to the bike repairman. His mom did all the talking. She explained the problems with the bike and discussed the price of the repair with the repairman. The kid just stood there. Why couldn't he explain the problem and make the repair decision himself, with his own money? Why was his mom even there at all?

Research and statistics confirm that this helplessness I witnessed in one teenage boy is widespread among children today. In her study of parenting advice in the 20th century,[5] Markella Rutherford finds that parents have come to consider schoolwork and, more generally, preparation for college, as their children's only "work." Parents today attempt to control their children's lives to an unprecedented extent, severely limiting their freedom outside the home. Thus, we have a generation of teenagers entering adulthood with very little idea how to get anything done for themselves in the world.

Kids get driven around everywhere, rarely venturing out on their own. In 1969, approximately half of all schoolchildren walked or bicycled to or from school, and 87 percent of those living within one mile of school walked or bicycled.[6] Today, less than 15 percent of children and adolescents use active modes of transportation.[7]

Many elementary schools have traffic jams in the early morning and late afternoon as dozens of cars line up to drop off or pick up children. The queues are often 10 minutes long or more. At pickup time, the kids hang out by the cars the whole time breathing in the noxious fumes, when they could be getting exercise walking home in the fresh air. For those who can't walk or ride to school for one reason or other, taking school buses is a diminishing option due to deep budget cuts. Although this is equivalent to being driven by parents from the point of view of exercise, it does enhance neighbor relations among the kids who ride the bus together every day.

Most teens in America have never held a job of any kind. In 2010, about 25 percent of the nation's 16- to 19-year-olds worked; in contrast, more than 50 percent of this age group worked in 1978.[8] This is a steady, long-term trend, not a sudden downturn due to the recession prevailing in 2010. Many common jobs for youth of decades earlier, such as newspaper delivery, cutting lawns, shoe shining, and retail clerk, have all but vanished. In contrast to children of older generations, most children of today enter adulthood with no idea how to work and no experience managing the money they earn.

At home, the time children spend on household chores has diminished markedly. According to research on how children spend their time, 9-to 12-year-old children spent 42 percent less time on household chores in 2003 than they did in 1981.[9] If comparable data existed for a period decades before 1981, it's highly likely the drop would be substantially greater.

Children are spending more time doing homework than they did decades ago, and they're not taking as much responsibility to do it on their own. A recent study showed that 43 percent of parents have done their kids' homework for them at least once.[10] That's not teaching. It's just cheating, pure and simple, perpetrated by parents.

When parents hover over their children, they're impeding a very fundamental urge. "Kids want to crawl and then run and then ride their bikes and finally drive their cars," Madeline Levine writes in *The Price of Privilege*. "Psychologists agree that this push toward activity, curiosity, and exploration is innate. . . . The need to experience a sense of control over things that affect our lives is universal."[11]

Parents and children typically engage in a battle for control. Given their built-in advantages (they buy the food, own the house, drive the car, etc.), parents usually win. Unfortunately, children pay a big price when they lose this battle. They come to believe that they are not capable of exerting influence over things in their own lives that matter to them.

Back when I was a kid, parents used to hold up "self-reliance" as a goal for their children. They used to boast about how their son walked to school with his friends every day, or how their daughter worked as a babysitter, saved her money, and bought her own bike.

My parents did a good job of fostering self-reliance in my sister and me. They made us walk with friends to and from school—more than a mile each way—starting in first grade. My dad had us work at his pharmacy from the age of 9 or 10, not because we were poor, but because he saw work and saving money as fundamental virtues. We each had regular chores to do around the house. I was responsible for cleaning the cats' litter box, taking the garbage to the garage every night, and cutting the grass in our yard, while my sister helped my mother with laundry and cooking. We had a lot less homework back then, but when my sister and I did it, we always did it completely by ourselves. My dad gave me free access to his lumber and non-power tools and he taught me basic carpentry skills to help my neighborhood friends and I build our own forts and furniture. He beamed when he came home from work each day and saw the stuff we had slapped together.

My parents left us on our own to play with our friends, so my friends and I organized our own sports games practically every day. We decided who would play, what we would play, where we would play it, we created custom rules for each day's varying circumstances, and we settled our own disputes.

There's nothing keeping parents today from teaching their kids self-reliance other than the prevailing culture of parenting. I recommend that parents rebel from this culture and encourage their kids to do things for themselves.

Parents' Time with Children

Studies show that parents, both mothers and fathers, are spending more time with their children than they did back in the 1960s, '70s, and '80s, when we parents were children. They also show a big shift in how parents spend time with children. A comprehensive review of all this research can be found in *The Rug Rat Race* by Gary and Valerie Ramey.[12]

There is good news and bad news in these numbers and the details behind them.

The good news is the fundamental fact that more hours with children means that parents are investing more time in their kids. This is quite impressive given that fact that all parents, mothers in particular, are spending more hours per week working than they did years ago. These increased hours with children and at work are accounted for mostly by decreases in time spent doing household chores and free time.

In general, children who spend more time with their parents are healthier and do better in school. Later in life, as adults, they are less likely to commit crimes, they attain a higher educational level, and they earn more money. In addition, children who spend more time with their parents are likely to have better relationships with them when they become adults.

In short, it's hard to argue against parents spending more time with their children.

The bad news is in the details of where parents are allocating their time with their children. The data show that parents are spending a lot more time "traveling" with kids or chauffeuring them, and supervising their activities. They are also spending more "educational" time with their kids, which is probably the time they spend helping their children with homework.

It is interesting to note that the increase in hours devoted to children is much more pronounced for older children than for younger children. *The Rug Rat Race* seizes on this fact to conclude that the increase in childcare time is due to parents' efforts to get their children into better colleges. Taken together, all these facts indicate that parents' highest priority is maximizing some notion of their children's future lives. They are "hovering" over their children like never before to assure that they have the best possible credentials for college.

The National KidsDay Meaningful Time Survey, conducted for the Boys & Girls Clubs of America in 2002, indicates that children and parents differ sharply as to what is quality time spent between them.[13] In essence, the survey shows that, although parents think that education-related time spent with children is quality time (the survey calls this "meaningful time"), children prefer fun time by a margin of 49 percent to 35 percent, while parents prefer education-related time by a margin of 62 percent to 35 percent. Parents tend to want to enrich their parenting experience, whereas children desire to feel wanted and supported. Clearly, the increased time parents are spending with their children is not being allocated as children would like.

How I Didn't Teach Nico to Ride His Bike Without Training Wheels

Yes, Nico's having a wonderful time riding his bike without training wheels.

Nico's the least coordinated of our sons. He runs awkwardly and can't hit a tennis ball with a racket to save his life. And yet, at the tender age of 3 years and 10 months, he learned how to ride his bike without training wheels.

I'm super proud of him, but actually, I can't really take any credit for teaching him.

The only person who taught Nico is Nico. Seriously. Other than the last 20 minutes or so, when Marco and I repeatedly yelled "Pedal!!!" and "Keep moving!!!," no one taught Nico any bike riding skills.

So, how did this not-very-coordinated 3-year-old accomplish this amazing feat almost all on his own? After all, most kids don't graduate from training wheels until at least the age of 5.

The answer is that he lives in a great environment for learning how to ride a bike. In fact, I'd say most 3-year-olds—even yours (!?!)—would be riding a bike without training wheels with barely any instruction if they had Nico's same situation.

Here are the components of his environment that enabled him to teach himself to ride a bike:

Lots of kids' wheeled vehicles in the garage: We don't put cars in our garage. It's all toys and storage, and the kids' wheeled vehicle inventory is impressive—two two-wheeled scooters, one three-wheeled scooter, two plastic trikes with big front wheels, a balance bike (no pedals or training wheels), roller skates and roller blades, a skateboard, and a few bikes of different sizes with training wheels and without. We have all of these because we have three boys, and our oldest went through most of these first.

A very smooth concrete driveway: When we moved into our present house three years ago, one of the first things I did was to remove the bumpy pavers and have a smooth concrete driveway installed. This may seem like a trivial renovation, even wasteful, but no change has had more of a positive impact on my kids' play lives. Regarding bike riding, it opened the possibility for my kids to roll around casually every day, right from our garage.

A calm, smooth street: Our block has few cars passing through it. In fact, practically the only cars that drive down it belong to people on our block. Also, our street was repaved last year, so its surface went from very uninviting for small wheels to very inviting.

An older brother who rides his bike a lot: We consider Marco, age 7, to be much more coordinated than Nico. He didn't start biking without training wheels until he was 5 because the house we lived in then didn't have nearly as good an environment for learning. However, since he started two years ago, he's turned into a great cyclist. He rides 1 1/2 miles to and from school every day, and from this foundation, he's started doing some adult-grade cycling this summer, including a 34-mile bike ride and a 1,700-foot mountain climb with me.

Freedom to play unsupervised: Nico and Marco play unsupervised quite a bit. We even let them ride bikes on the street in front of our house, with an adult checking in frequently. When that happens, we usually have one of those "Slow, Children at Play" signs in the middle of the street. That may seem super scary to many parents, but we did not give this freedom all of a sudden. We increased it incrementally over the years, as they gained more "independence skills." At this point, Nico's very good about watching for cars and getting out of the way when they come.

Lots of free time: We have no television or video games inside the house, and we don't schedule many activities for our kids. So, they're outside in our yard and neighborhood for hours every day, having fun. Really. . .

The story of Nico learning to ride a bike without training wheels starts with him being in our driveway and street a lot, watching Marco riding his bike, first with training wheels, then not. Of course, Nico had a strong desire to do the same. There were two years of trial and error on all the wheeled vehicles in our garage, culminating in the training-wheels bike and the balance bike. When I saw he'd mastered the latter, I knew he was ready for a two-wheeler and encouraged him to try it one day. Using the skills he'd mastered one day at a time, he was riding down our block on his own within 15 or 20 minutes!

Now, he rides in front of our house with his brother Marco frequently. When we ride as a family to somewhere close by, he bikes along with us, rather than riding in a trailer, as he used to do. He's well on his way to riding to school or to friends' houses self-sufficiently, as Marco does.

This is a story of thousands of experiments, practically all initiated by Nico over a couple of years, to try something new and harder. It would have been foolish for adults to try to control this process. Alison Gopnik makes the point very eloquently in *The Philosophical Baby*[14] that kids are great trial and error experimenters, all by themselves. Nico did a fabulous job himself. All we did was set the table for him.

What Approach Should Parents Take?

Given the perils of controlling kids' lives to the extent that most parents do today, how would I recommend parents allocate their time and attention? I would not advocate that we go back to the way parents used to be and spend less time with our children. Children benefit greatly from having parents involved in their lives, provided that the involvement doesn't conflict with their own desires.

Instead, I think parents should opt for an approach I call "facilitated self-reliance." Whereas parents today tend to hover over their children well into the teenage years, I'd like to see parents step more to the side, but remain present, as our children get older. We should become facilitators for our children to help them find their own identities and achieve their highest potential while modeling some absolute values for safety, morality, and achievement. We should bring our children into stimulating and challenging situations, model behavior for them, and then provide them with the opportunity to take over more and more of these situations on their own.

Certainly, when our kids are first born, they are helpless, so we need to totally control their lives. However, from the moment they start walking, we constantly have important decisions to make about how to deal with their quests for independence. These quests, if they're nurtured properly, become great opportunities for our children to mature and achieve mastery in the world.

As Rutherford points out in her study, promoting self-reliance used to be a primary goal of parenting, but it has almost completely been replaced by parents' desire to focus their children's energies on preparing for college. Although I agree that preparing for college is worthy, it shouldn't be emphasized to the exclusion of self-reliance.

The kinds of lessons a child can learn from having some measure of autonomy will help them succeed in their adult years. Social skills, problem-solving skills, and creativity are byproducts of self-reliance. In addition, to the extent that being self-reliant increases their competence in dealing with the world, children will enjoy their childhood years more.

Having self-reliant kids can take a big load off of parents as well, enabling them to enjoy themselves more. Many studies have found that taking care of their children makes parents unhappy.[15] Like many of these researchers, I speculate that this is a recent phenomenon—meaning parenting "job satisfaction" has been decreasing over the past decades to the point where it is now. One of the most prominent reasons offered for this unhappiness in parenting is that micromanaging kids' lives is no fun. It's nerve-racking to manage someone else's life so tightly, especially when they resent your doing it.

On the other hand, parents and their self-reliant children develop relationships of mutual respect. Over time, because their parents give them opportunities to make some of their own decisions, children gain an ability to make good ones. Thus, parents grow to trust their children more and more.

The Incremental Approach to Facilitating Self-Reliance

"How is it that you feel so comfortable letting Marco be in your front yard without watching him?"

A mom asked me this question last year. It really froze me. I mean, I hadn't really thought about how we had become comfortable giving him so much freedom.

I discussed "Marco's village" in Chapter 14. He was 6 1/2 years old when I made the map of his village shown on page 161, and he regularly roamed an area within about two blocks of our house. Most kids' home range—the range they regularly and comfortably inhabit every day—is limited to the boundaries of their yard, and some aren't even allowed out of their house alone.

Still, this mom's query got me to really think about how we could let him do that, while so many parents of kids Marco's age couldn't bear the thought that their kids are outside alone.

How did we get here?

In short, we ended up here after an awful lot of repetition and incremental adjustments every day, right outside our front door. Perla and I didn't just wake up when Marco turned 6 and say, "OK, Marco, it's time for you to start wandering the neighborhood on your own." Rather, we started taking steps when he started walking, and we've worked practically daily on his independence skills. Although he's been our focus, all this "work" has made an important impact on my wife and me, as well as on our neighbors.

When he was 2, we let Marco chase balls down on the sidewalk in front of our house. This wasn't entirely comfortable, and sometimes I had to yell and/or chase him down to keep him from really endangering himself. However, he learned daily from these experiences, and I'm sure that he became a bit better than other 2-year-olds at self-control close to a street.

When Marco was 3, I took him bike riding in our neighborhood. He would sometimes get out of control on his training-wheels bike, and once again, I had to yell and chase him down quite a bit. Eventually, though, he got pretty good at bike riding close to cars.

The next year, when he was 4, we started to let him play for very short amounts of time in front of our house without our watching. We lost him once and panicked until we found him behind a bush in our next-door neighbors' yard. We reprimanded him sharply, but in retrospect, I realize that this was an important teachable moment. He began to understand how his small bit of freedom came with some responsibility. He also started riding his bike on the street with me then, and I gave him a little space to roam away from me.

At 5, Marco began riding his bike in the street without training wheels. Little by little, I let him ride farther and farther away from me, and now, he rides 1 1/2 miles to school every day, sometimes with me, and sometimes with our nanny. He's gotten quite good at riding that route, so good that I think he'll be ready to ride on his own very soon.

My main point here is that every day, we've kept in mind independence and self-reliance as goals for Marco. Every day, he's learned and gotten better at being independent. Sure, we've made some mistakes, but these mistakes were never huge ones because we gave only a tiny bit more rope every day.

I'll offer an analogy. When you start teaching your children to recognize letters in the hope that they will one day learn to read, you take an incremental approach. Next, you try to get them to recognize a few two-letter words like "no" or "go." Then, you teach them different three-letter words that have one letter different, like "man" and "can" and "fan." You don't wait until they're 6, throw a book in their lap, and expect them to read.

Likewise, independence skills require constant, continuous improvement. The word that comes to mind for me is the Japanese word "kaizen." Literally, it means "change for the better," but the term has taken on incredible importance as a philosophy of manufacturing at Japanese companies like Toyota. The idea there is to scrutinize every detail of the automobile manufacturing process every day, and make small, incremental improvements based on that scrutiny every day. After many years practicing kaizen in the 1960s, '70s, and '80s, Toyota ended up with manufacturing processes that were wildly superior to American car manufacturers.

Today, Marco is on the way to being the Toyota of his neighborhood in independence skills. (This is partially because many other parents of kids his age don't even attempt to teach these skills.) Besides roaming within a fairly broad area around our house, he even occasionally rides his bike to and from his school by himself. I'm very proud of him. Not only do I have confidence in him, but he also has a great deal of confidence in himself.

However, I can't bear to think right now of him riding on the busy street by our house, El Camino Real, on his own. In addition, even though he can read very simple, short books, I can't imagine his reading a Harry Potter book on his own right now. Both will come at the right time. We'll get there.

Suggestions for Facilitating Self-Reliance

How can parents support their elementary school-aged and older kids in gaining independent lives in their neighborhoods? The key for parents is to remain relevant to these activities, but more as resources and peers to their children than as masters controlling them. Note that the foundation for these activities is encapsulated in the recommendations of the previous chapter on creating a vibrant neighborhood life for young children.

Teach Kids How to Play Pickup Sports Games

Many of my best childhood memories involve playing pickup games with no adults around. Yes, I played organized sports—Little League baseball, for instance—but those experiences simply don't compare with pickup games with my neighborhood friends.

I would argue that pickup ball is both more fun and better for children's social and intellectual development. The legendary child development theorist Jean Piaget wrote about how children develop moral reasoning through their independent game playing in *The Moral Judgment of the Child*.[16] Piaget observed early 20th-century Swiss children playing marbles, progressing beyond a state of "moral realism," in which they just accept rules without understanding the need for them or the logic behind them. As they played games where they encountered new unforeseen situations, they came to their own understanding of why rules are actually needed. They grappled with issues of fairness, equity, and the administrative cost of creating and applying new rules. Piaget argued that experiences like this play a vital role in helping children grow to a more mature stage of moral development.

Here are some of the developmentally valuable tasks kids undertake for a pickup game that they don't for adult-organized sports:

- Decide what to play
- Recruit players
- Decide where to play
- Improvise rules
- Settle disputes
- Decide how to conclude the game
- Bend the rules for less able kids

So how do we parents help to get pickup games happening in our neighborhoods? Marco is just beginning to understand how to play complex games like baseball or basketball with his friends, and without the help of adults. He plays very informal, brief street hockey, soccer, and baseball games at recess at school almost every day, and he occasionally plays street hockey in front of our house.

His biggest challenge for playing pickup sports in our neighborhood will be recruiting enough kids to play a decent game. In spite of the fact that we have a large number of kids nearby, very few are available at any given time to spontaneously come out and play. To overcome this startup problem, I've been thinking about scheduling a kids' pickup street hockey game or two on weekend mornings. I would try to avoid playing if possible, but I do envision helping the kids choose teams, set up the "rink," and establish rules—hopefully, just at the outset, to get them going. In my childhood neighborhood, my friends and I had older kids do this for us, but in my current one, I'm attempting to start this from scratch, with no older kids to help out.

My guess is that in the beginning, at least, it'll take a lot of behind-the-scenes work by me, such as checking with parents for common free time among kids and getting games started. However, my goal is to get the kids to a self-sustaining habit of pickup games with as little adult intervention as possible. Some fights, bumps, and bruises would all be a part of this. I'm OK with it as long as it doesn't get out of hand, and I hope other parents will be, too. Can I pull it off? We'll see. . .

Give Kids Chores

As I mentioned earlier, it is common today for parents to consider children's home-work their only "work" around the house, and to excuse them of most, if not all, household chores. I strongly believe that this leads children to think of their respon-sibilities much too narrowly. They should think of themselves as full members of their households, not mere consumers of their parents' and babysitters' services. As they do chores more and more, they'll gain mastery that they can apply beyond their home. For instance, the skills they learn helping mom or dad paint the bathroom will come in handy when they want to paint their own fort.

In addition, doing chores at home can be kids' first paying job, so that they learn about how to earn money. Children should have to earn spending money through completing household chores, rather than simply being given an unearned allow-ance. The best system, I believe, is a set allowance for regular chores, and then peri-odic special projects for extra money. These special projects help children understand better that they're getting paid for the work that they do. They also have the potential to inspire children to dream up other tasks they can do for money. In fact, parents should encourage this sort of entrepreneurial thinking because it can lead to more serious, and lucrative, entrepreneurial projects outside the home.

My wife and I have just tried an experiment in this regard: We're paying Marco for every vegetable that he grows and harvests from our garden. We pay different rates for different vegetables (peas, tomatoes, beets, etc.). This scheme has made him very motivated to learn how to manage our garden to get the best possible yield. It's also helped him quite a bit with his arithmetic. Plus, it's a great way to keep him outside.

So, how old should children be when they first start doing household chores for money? Of course, every child is different, but they tend to acquire a sufficient sense of responsibility and an interest in money in the early elementary school years.

Help Kids Find a Job or Start a Business

The gardening deal we have with Marco, described above, is the foundation of a business for him. He has zero costs, but I could envision telling him he needs to buy his own supplies like fertilizer and gardening tools when he gets a bit older. In addition, I could let him sell extra produce to neighbors. This would be a tremendous learning experience, teaching him how to manage costs, sell and market, manage orders and inventory, and provide customer service.

The classic lemonade (or homemade cookie) stand teaches young kids the basics of pricing strategy, as well as sales and customer service skills. Kids learn a lot more if they have to buy the ingredients and / or make the items from scratch because then, they're basically running a whole business with costs as well as revenues.

As kids get older, they can go door to door selling their services to neighbors. Car washing, gardening, and babysitting are examples of services that children can do that are in constant high demand. Parents can "set up" their children to run these businesses by helping them build those skills at home first, then helping them with sales tactics (how much to charge, who to approach, how to approach them, etc.). Of course, this bolsters neighborhood relations and familiarity as well.

My neighbor friend Krist recently set his 10-year-old daughter up in a business rather than just giving her money. She wanted some new Barbies and accessories, and he told her that she needed to earn the money to buy them. He knew that she was very good at painting the faces of younger kids like her sister and her friends, so, one day he helped her bring her face painting supplies and two chairs to a nearby park. She made more than $20 in just a couple of hours, and a few days later, she and a friend brought all those things to the park without any adult help. After that second day painting faces, she earned the $35 she needed to buy everything she wanted!

When kids get into their teen years, they can get a job at a local business. All jobs, however menial, teach responsibility, the value of work, the value of money, and time management skills. Children these days usually need their parents' help to find a job or business opportunity. If a parent knows the owner of a neighborhood retail store well, that can be a good place to try. Retailers often need people to clean, stock merchandise, or wait on customers.

Help Kids Establish a Nearby Nature Hangout

I described how I've helped to establish a nature hangout at the creek by our house for my kids and neighbor kids. Finding such a place just isn't possible for many urban-based kids, but if there's any decent nature within walking distance of home, it can be very worthwhile trying to establish a kid's hangout there.

Numerous studies show that increased time in nature makes children healthier both physically and emotionally.[17] Unfortunately, many parents' idea of exposing kids to nature is packing them into a car for a long drive to a big park once every month or two. However, when we consider all the research that proves the value of free play, the inescapable conclusion is that children need to have a place in nature where they can eventually go unsupervised.

This should not be hard work. Children naturally develop a deep affinity for nature if they are exposed to it often, from an early age. This is one of the messages of *The Last Child in the Woods*, by Richard Louv. Parents of preschoolers should take them often to one particular wild natural setting that is, ideally, within a mile of home, and they should walk or bike there rather than drive, if possible. Bodies of water like creeks or ponds are excellent destinations because there's so much going on there, but places with climbable trees (yes, let them climb!) can be very good destinations as well. If children go to one nature spot enough, they will develop a deep bond with it.

As children enter the elementary school years, their parents should permit them to wander off and explore areas on their own. Slowly but surely, they'll become more comfortable with that place until they can finally roam there with no adult supervision.

Encourage Independent Roaming

At what age can children start roaming more than a block on their own, beyond the sight of parents? Obviously, the answer to this question is dependent on many factors. In my neighborhood, kids as young as 6 (including Marco) have wandered in our creek with no adults around. The answer depends on the amount of traffic on the streets in a neighborhood, the overall feeling of safety, and the maturity level of the child.

Most parents will, to some extent, fear the prospect of their children roaming on their own. Some amount of fear is natural, given the real dangers to children in the world. However, parental fear should be based on fact, not irrational distortions. Busy streets are definitely a very large danger to children. However, in most neighborhoods, violent crime is not a big danger. As I've noted before, stranger abductions are extremely rare.

One important thing that parents have control over is the level of independence skills of their children. Children can begin to develop these as soon as they can walk. I discussed "The Incremental Approach" earlier. The children in my neighborhood who were going to the creek at age 6 were roaming up and down the sidewalk at age 4, and riding their bikes around the block at age 5.

In the next chapter, I'll discuss how parents can co-opt tweens' and teens' interest in technology to make them highly competent roamers in their neighborhoods, far more competent than children of decades ago ever were.

Playborhoods and Kids With Special-Needs

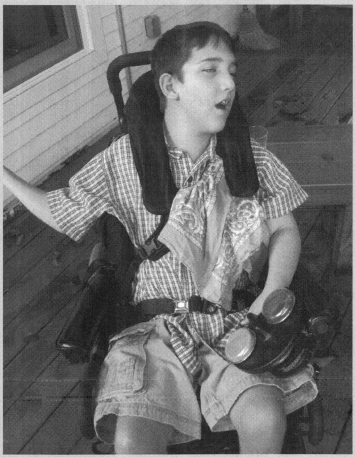

Ben hits the ball and strike buttons on the right to "call 'em as he sees 'em" for neighborhood Wiffle ball games.

In a Playborhood in Burlington, Vt., Ben, an 11-year-old boy with cerebral palsy, can't walk or talk, and his sight and hearing are somewhat impaired. In spite of these disabilities, he umpires Wiffle ball games with the aid of two switches in his wheelchair arm that he can hit with a finger to play the words "strike" and "ball."

Certainly, the neighborhood kids care for Ben and understand his limitations, but they're not above arguing with him like any other member of his team. His dad, Michael, told me about a boy who argued with Ben over a called strike just a few days ago. Perhaps Ben should get a new switch to play the word "ejected!"

BEN'S SPECIAL BIKE Ben's bike enables him to zoom through his neighborhood with friends when someone else pedals it. The girl pedaling it here, at right, is his sister.

Wheelchair-bound Ben also rides a special bike, with the help of one of his siblings or parents. The girl doing the driving in the photo here is his 8-year-old sister, Madeline. So, he's able to ride around his neighborhood, which is plentiful with kids and activities, and also around town with his family when they go on bike outings, rather than being isolated in a van.

Getting to know the situation with Ben in Burlington brings back memories for me. In my childhood neighborhood, when my friends and I played pickup sports games, we almost always invited Bobby, a mentally handicapped boy, and David, a deaf boy, to play with us. We created special rules for them to make sure they enjoyed playing with us. For example, Bobby wouldn't want to play softball with us again if he never got a hit, so he got as many strikes as he wanted and anything he hit was fair—meaning he had no foul balls. It was an easy compromise, and everyone had fun.

What is it about Playborhoods that make them egalitarian havens? Fundamentally, I think that, the closer activity is to homes, the more *opportunity* there is to put all residents on an equal footing, so to speak.

Any location that requires driving puts drivers in a position of power vis-à-vis passengers. They decide where to go and when. Obviously all children are prohibited from driving, so being driven disempowers them, but physically handicapped and mentally handicapped children have additional reasons to prefer staying close to home. They often have more difficulty adapting to new places for a variety of reasons. Physically, they may have problems navigating new obstacles like steps and tight spaces. Mentally and emotionally, they may feel less secure if they are surrounded by strangers. This means physically and mentally disabled kids—aka kids with "special-needs"—can reap great benefits from a Playborhood, gaining self-reliance and a sense of community.

Beyond this, though, is the fact that non-special-needs kids can benefit greatly from playing with special-needs kids in a Playborhood. I know that my friends and I thought very deeply about our goals when we played pickup sports with Bobby and David. We had to balance our desire to have our own fun and our desire that *they* have fun, too. So, every time we invited them to play with us, and every time we made a special rule for them and applied it, we grappled with the tradeoff between our own self-interest and egalitarianism.

Similarly, Ben's siblings and neighbors probably grapple with this tradeoff every day. Would someone with perfect eyesight, the ability to walk, and the ability to talk make a better umpire? Certainly, but is it really important to have the "best" umpire possible?

Ben's siblings and neighborhood friends believe that his umpiring provides an interesting new dimension to Wiffle ball games that a boring, perfect umpire wouldn't. And along the way, the kids of the block are absorbing life lessons about tolerance, difference, and acceptance. I envy them. I wish my kids had a kid like Ben around to play with.

Let Them Roam with Mobile Phones

If you just read the previous three chapters, you might feel like I've taken you to Beaver Cleaver's 1950s neighborhood in a time machine—or that I've wanted to. I've painted a picture of how you can have your kids playing outside in their neighborhood, becoming more self-reliant day by day, consuming very little Internet, video games, or TV. Regardless of whether you find that image appealing, it's just not sustainable through the teen years because digital electronics are too deeply embedded in teen culture, social life in particular.

In this chapter, I'll bring you back to the 2010s. In case you aren't grateful already, I aim to make you grateful that you're raising your kids here and now. The worst effects of digital technology are behind us, I believe. Enough research has been done of its negative impact on very young children that those of us who pay attention will pull back. We won't leave our kids under 2 alone in front of a TV, and we'll limit their exposure to all media in the years after that. We won't let our kids consume anywhere near eight hours per day. We get it.

Beyond the fact that we're limiting total exposure, what excites me far more is that the most important technologies for the next decade are mobile. The coolest technologies for kids five or 10 years ago were tethered to the wall—video games, DVD players, and desktop computers connected to the Internet. So, kids sat inside their houses for hours a day, not moving around, and not interacting face to face with other people.

Mobile technologies can do the opposite. They encourage roaming about the world. And although they are often used today as a replacement for face-to-face interactions, new mobile applications in the coming years will increasingly encourage them. We can actually guide our kids' mobile phone use to support their outdoor play and their self-reliance. Seriously, we can begin to embrace digital technology, or at least one significant part of it, for our older kids' lives. Skeptical? Intrigued? We'll get there, but first, I need to step back and discuss tweens' and teens' urge to roam, which is so well supported by mobile phones.

Tweens, Teens, and Roaming

Do you remember wanting to rebel against your parents when you were a tween or teenager? Do you remember the impulse inside you to get away from them and explore? We might be ashamed to admit that we had these feelings now because we're parents, but having them is perfectly normal for older children. In fact, older children need to assert some measure of independence to learn how to become competent young adults.

This yearning for independence has been expressed by children throughout history via physical roaming. Children find new places and encounter new people, so that they become able to transcend the world their parents present to them, and they learn a great deal in the process. In her memoir of her childhood in Pittsburgh in the mid-20th century, *An American Childhood*, Annie Dillard writes:

> I walked. My mother had given me the freedom of the streets as soon as I could say our telephone number. I walked and memorized the neighborhood. I made a mental map and located myself upon it. At night in bed I rehearsed the small world's scheme and set challenges: Find the store using backyards only. Imagine a route from the school to my friend's house.[1]

In his outrageously funny memoir of his childhood in the '50s and '60s in Des Moines, Iowa, *The Life and Times of the Thunderbolt Kid*, Bill Bryson writes of how he and his friends in the early 1960s often toed the line between mischief and creativity in their quest to kill time:

> We were extremely good at just fooling around. Saturday mornings were primarily devoted to attaining an elevated position—the roofs of office buildings, the windows at ends of long corridors in the big hotels—and dropping soft or wet things on shoppers below. We spent many happy hours, too, roaming through the behind-the-scenes parts of department stores and office buildings, looking in broom closets and stationery cabinets, experimenting with steamy valves in boiler rooms, poking though boxes in storerooms.

The trick was never to behave furtively, but to act as if you didn't realize you were in the wrong place. If you encountered an adult, you could escape arrest or detention by immediately asking a dumb question: "Excuse me, mister, is this the way to Mr. Mackenzie's office?" or "Can you tell me where the men's room is, please?" This approach never failed. With a happy chuckle the apprehending custodian would guide us back to daylight and set us on our way with a pat on the head, unaware that under our jackets were 13 rolls of duct tape, two small fire extinguishers, an adding machine, one semipornographic calendar from his office wall, and a really lethal staple gun.[2]

It's clear that Dillard and Bryson were learning important life skills in the course of their roaming.

Unfortunately, children of today hardly roam at all.

Beyond the impact of parents' prohibitions, children are less likely to choose to roam on their own now due to their very short attention spans, acquired through extensive electronic media exposure. In fact, many children today mimic the adventures of Dillard and Bryson via their online activities. They participate in chat rooms with an anonymous ID and a fake persona, participate on massively multiplayer online role-playing games like World of Warcraft, or surf Web sites their parents would not approve of. In the meantime, they miss out on a lot of real-world skill building.

Active Neighborhood Life as the Foundation for Roaming

Children's quest for independence starts as soon as they can walk. Certainly, it intensifies in the tween years and even more in the teen years, but the skills and habits that children accumulate before those years strongly influence their behavior later on.

Tween children with an active neighborhood life go to neighborhood friends' houses alone, negotiate play, and even return home on their own. They might walk or ride their bikes to school independently if the trip is short and safe. They might walk to a neighborhood retail store and buy something.

Children who successfully do these things earn their parents' trust, and thus the opportunity for more open-ended freedom. Over time, their parents give them more and more open-ended instructions. What started as "Come right home from school. Don't stop anywhere on the way home!" might evolve into "It's OK if you stop at Sandy's on the way home. If you do that, just ask her mom to call me." Later, the parent might give a lot more freedom, saying something like "You can go where you want after school, as long as you don't cross the major road. Also, be home by 6."

How can a parent know when a child is ready for more freedom? If parents continue the incremental approach for neighborhood freedom, they'll never have to make a big, highly uncertain decision concerning their children's independence. Competence for children, as well as trust for parents, builds up over countless experiences and many years.

Mobile Phones and Independence

Of course, even with a highly competent child and very trusting parents, unexpected problems or opportunities might emerge while a child is roaming. For instance, a child's bicycle tire might blow out on the way home from school, and he might call his mom to get picked up; a parent might get caught in a bad traffic jam and ask the child to stay at her friend's house a little longer; or a child might ask if he can accept an impromptu invitation from friends to go to a basketball game for the evening. For cases like these and many more, mobile phones have emerged as indispensable communications tools between parents and independent children. Termed an "electronic tether" by critics, a mobile phone link between parents and children enables them to communicate anywhere, anytime.

In fact, the mobile phone has become many older children's primary tool for achieving independence from their parents. A Pew Internet and American Life Project study titled *Teens and Mobile Phones* highlights independence and freedom as the most important impact of a mobile phone on teens' lives: 94 percent of teen mobile phone owners agreed with the statement "My cell phone gives me more freedom because I can stay in touch with my parents no matter where I am." One high school girl explained, "I think [a cell phone] gives you more freedom in the sense that if you're trying to get permission to go someplace, it helps to say, 'I'll have my phone, you can call me if you need to,' and then it makes parents feel more secure. Which is how I think it gives you more freedom."[3]

Practically all parents agree that mobile phones enable them to grant more independence. The Pew study reports that "98% of parents of cell-owning teens say a major reason their child has the phone is that they can be in touch no matter where the teen is."[4]

Mobile Phones and Parent-Child Intimacy

This increased independence afforded to teens by mobile phones has not resulted in more distant relationships. On the contrary, mobile phones have enabled a deeper level of intimacy between parents and children. In Pew's Networked Family report, 47 percent of adults reported that mobile phones increased the quality of their communications with household members, whereas only 4 percent reported a decrease. Another 47 percent thought mobile phones made no difference.[5]

Similarly, adult respondents feel that the Internet and mobile phones have made their family today closer than the family they grew up in decades ago: 25 percent feel this way, 60 percent feel that these technologies haven't made much difference in this regard, and only 11 percent feel that their family today is not as close as their childhood family because of new technologies.[6]

Most people would readily agree that mobile phones make quick transactional communications easier—for instance, messages like "I'll be home 15 minutes late." However, these surveys find an increase in the *quality* of family communications, not just the quantity.

Give Them Mobile Phones Early

Taken together, the results from the Pew surveys mentioned in the previous two sections indicate that mobile phones result in more independence for teens and a closer relationship between children and their parents. That's a very desirable outcome, and presents a good argument for giving mobile phones to teens.

In this section, though, I'll argue that children should be given mobile phones before the teen years. Mobile phone usage among tweens and teens has been increasing significantly in recent years, and the average age of first phone has been decreasing. As of September 2009, 58 percent of 12-year-olds had a cell phone, compared with 73 percent of 13-year-olds.[7] No recent data are available on when the average kid gets a mobile phone, but from these data, we can infer that the age is around 11 or 12 and dropping.

I won't offer an exact age when to get a child a mobile phone, as this is such a subjective decision, but I will offer a few issues to guide you. First, you can start to think about getting your child one when he or she can manage it without losing it. Second, a child should be able to operate a mobile phone interface well. Most young kids are good at feeling their way around the interface of an electronic gadget, but to use a device that has so much communications power, they should be able to actually read and comprehend most or all of the interface. Of course, children will need to be a bit older to understand how to operate more complex phones like smartphones.

The possible health risk to children's brains from frequent mobile phone use is mentioned by some parents as a reason to postpone giving one to them. Research on this question—in particular, whether mobile phone use is associated with brain cancer—is inconclusive at this time. There is a particular interest in mobile phones' effect on children because their brains are not fully developed, and are perhaps more vulnerable to the radiation emitted by mobile phones. Currently, a research project called "Mobi-Kids"[8] is focusing on this question. Given research results to date, it is extremely unlikely that researchers would recommend zero exposure to mobile phones. The question is whether very high amounts of exposure have any negative effect. If parents have a concern about this risk even before any conclusive evidence is reported, they can insist that their children always use a headset to talk rather than holding their phones to their ears.

Another factor in deciding when to give children mobile phones is cost and financial responsibility. Conventional adult plans can get very costly if limits are exceeded. Children sometimes run up very high bills on these plans, even if their parents warn them not to do so. So, mobile phone carriers have begun to provide children's plans through which parents can limit calling minutes, text messages, and megabytes downloaded per month. Most children's plans also offer parents control over the time of day the phone can be used and whether the phone can access "inappropriate" Web content.

Given that these children's plans exist and are getting more and more sophisticated, I would advocate that children get mobile phones as soon as the other two conditions are met: when they can manage a phone without losing it, and when they can navigate its interface pretty well. These conditions imply an age around 8 to 9 years old, but, of course, it depends on the child.

The other important question to consider is what kind of mobile phone to get a child. Smartphones with GPS applications hold tremendous promise for increasing children's competence in the physical world and enjoyment of it, but they are relatively complex to operate and expensive, both because of purchase price and because of the plans that must accompany them to fully utilize them. However, it's clear that smartphones are becoming more and more popular, and might eventually become the most common type of mobile phone. Much lower-priced smartphones and plans are certain to emerge in the next couple of years.

I should make one more comment about the price of smartphones. Although they are expensive and will not come down to the price of entry-level phones anytime soon, they have tremendous utility beyond the phone itself, so they can substitute for other devices that parents might buy for their kids like video game consoles or iPods.

Set Limits for Mobile Phones

You might get the idea that I'm an unqualified proponent of mobile phones for children. On the contrary, I'm critical of mobile phones for children for much the same reason that I'm critical of all electronics technologies for them. Mobile phones can immerse users in a virtual world, making the real world vanish from their consciousness.

For instance, when my teenage nieces and nephews come to my house and text their friends at our dinner table, it's as if their brains have left their bodies. They become zombies. I try to talk to them, but they have no idea what I'm saying or doing, and could care less. They're totally immersed in virtual conversations with their friends.

When they're talking or texting, mobile phone users are totally absorbed in a world apart from the real, physical world that the rest of us are inhabiting with them. This is because of the phenomenon of "location independence," in which the user's experience with the phone is completely independent of, even ignorant of, the place in which it's being used.

One study of 40 teens with an average age of 14 finds that they average 34 text messages per night after bedtime.[9] The texts are sent or received from 10 minutes to four hours after the teen goes to bed, and, on average, a teen was awoken once a night by a text. The study found correlations between electronic media use late at night and ADHD, mood swings, anxiety, depression and problems with thinking skills during the day.

This need to stay connected at all times can be deadly when a teen is driving. Pew's *Teens and Mobile Phones* reports that 52 percent of 16- to 17-year-olds admit to talking on a mobile phone while driving, and 34 percent admitted to texting while driving.[10] Both significantly increase the chances of an accident. A study from the

Virginia Tech Transportation Institute reports that the chance of an accident is 23 times greater when the driver is texting, as compared to an undistracted driver.[11]

So, clearly, children should not be allowed to use mobile phones anywhere and anytime they want. My view is that mobile phone use inside the home should be restricted—especially at mealtime or bedtime—or even totally prohibited. Of course, kids should be educated about never using mobile phones while driving, biking, or on busy streets.

Certainly, some parents might be tempted to say, "Screw it. The possible problems are too worrisome. I'm going to keep mobile phones away from my kids for as long as I can." This is the wrong approach, in my opinion. Children will demand and get their mobile phones eventually—they are just too important to tween and teen culture. If you get them phones early and set out good, explicit rules, you'll give your kids time to learn responsible mobile phone use before the teen years, when extreme social pressures and driving raise the stakes significantly. Besides, you'll be giving them a great tool to learn how to become more independent and self-reliant at an earlier age. And, as you'll see below, phones can offer new and exciting ways to interact with your neighborhood and the people in it.

Encourage Kids to Use GPS

If talking and texting on mobile phones turn users into zombies, GPS-based applications have the opposite effect. Users of these applications become hyper-aware of their surroundings, even more aware than people with no digital devices at all. That's because GPS-based applications are location *dependent*. In other words, experiences with these applications are tied to the physical environment and people nearby.

Here's how these applications work. A GPS chip in the mobile phone receives signals from multiple GPS satellites to calculate the position of the phone within 10 meters or so. The phone downloads map data from the Web to show its current location. GPS applications show that phone user on a map in relation to both fixed items (buildings, streets, parks, creeks, etc.) and other mobile phone users who are close by right now. In other words, these applications are all about where the user is physically relative to things around him or her. This makes them ideally suited for enhancing users' knowledge of the physical world around them, as well as for enhancing their enjoyment of it.

GPS-based applications on mobile phones will encourage children to roam, and to increase their competence in navigating on their own. Below I describe GPS application categories relevant to kids, along with particular recommendations for each.

Electronic Maps

As someone who is very proud of his sense of direction and his ability to find things on his own, I was initially resistant to the first navigation system I got in my new car back in 2004. My impression was that navigation systems were for directionally challenged people, much like people who are skilled at mental mathematical calculations think that calculators are for people who aren't good at math.

I quickly discovered after using my navigation system for a few weeks that I was dead wrong. My navigation system gave me a much deeper understanding of where I was at any particular time, giving me more ability to serendipitously find things in the course of a day driving around. After going to our initial destination, I found parks or restaurants I never knew about, and in the process of finding these, I often discovered whole areas I had known nothing about.

A mapping application on a smartphone can have an even more revolutionary impact on children's lives because their minds are much more open to using it than mine is. Because I lived for more than 40 years without any electronic mapping application, I will always have a bias toward relying on places I already know in my head. However, children who use a smartphone mapping application from their first years as roamers will develop new, more flexible ways of navigating and finding places. They will become more competent explorers than today's parents ever were. They will have a whole new impetus to discover new parts of their neighborhood on their own.

It's important to note that electronic mapping applications have far less potential to make children lazy in navigation than many claim calculators make children lazy in math. This is because the answer in a navigation problem, unlike in a math problem, can only be crudely represented on an electronic device. Once a user sees an "answer" that the mapping application provides on a map, he or she must still figure out how to get there on real streets with (or without) real street signs and landmarks. If the answer involves public transportation, he or she must still figure out how to buy tickets, get on the bus or train, and get off at the right spot. Because of this, utilizing an electronic mapping application always results in more learning about real-world places. Utilizing the number answer on a calculator requires far less mental work, so it results in very little learning.

Smartphone mapping applications like Google Maps enable users to do the following three fundamental tasks:

1) Find where they currently are on a map

2) Find places of interest in the vicinity of one's current location (e.g., find the closest locations with keyword "ice cream")

3) Get turn-by-turn directions from the user's current location to any other location (e.g., show me how to get from here to the park or from here to school). These directions can easily be changed from the default driving route to a pedestrian route or a public transit route.

Location-Based Games

Location-based games constitute an exciting new category of electronic games that use the real world as the game board. In other words, while a GPS-based phone is used to facilitate the game, users must navigate through the real world and interact with elements in it (like real people) to accomplish game objectives. These games are a great way to bring neighbor kids together for independent outdoor adventures close to home.

Geocaching is the most well known example of a location-based game, played by millions of people, many of whom are parents playing with their kids. Essentially, a geocaching app (like Geocaching Intro from Groundspeak on the iPhone) leads you to a geocache, or container, that has interesting items and a logbook inside it. Thousands of these have been left behind all over the United States and other countries by previous geocachers. Your phone can get you close to a geocache, but you'll always have some work to do to find it. You can take one of those items if you leave one of equal or greater value, and you should also make an entry in the logbook inside the cache.

In Seek 'n Spell, players with smartphones (iPhone or Android) gather in one place and start the game together. Appearing on each of their phones is a satellite map about two soccer fields big, then squares with letters on the map at different locations. When they start the game, players scatter to get to those letter squares on their phones. Players can make words with the letters they collect to get points.

I've played this game myself, and can testify that it gets you running, it forces you to explore a place very deeply, and it helps you have lots of fun with other people. This is a terrific game for your kids to play with neighbor kids, sort of like capture the flag or a pickup sports game, but with a technology component to appeal to their geeky side.

I participated in an experimental game called paparazzi in New York's Times Square in 2009. Teams of three took on the role of either a celebrity entourage (celebrity plus two body guards) or paparazzi. The paparazzi chased the celebrity entourages throughout Times Square, using maps on cell phones. We had a great time, got a lot of exercise, got to know each other very well, and learned a ton about the geography of Times Square, all in a couple of hours!

Some established video games are moving to blend their virtual worlds with the real world. For instance, Angry Birds is rolling out a new capability called "Magic Places" in which a player with a smartphone can unlock special game content like new birds and new levels at specific real-world locations. Players may even be able to exchange these items with other players they encounter in the real world by tapping phones.

I (right) and the woman on the left are protecting the celebrity, the guy behind us, from being photographed by "paparazzi" in Times Square. We really got into this location-based game!

As a genre of electronic games, location-based games are in their infancy, a tiny fraction of the entire electronic games market. However, I fully expect them to become an important force in children's lives in the coming decade. These games are beneficial for their children for the following reasons:

- They can be extremely engaging.
- They can substitute for non-location-based electronic games (e.g., console video games and computer games) that make kids sedentary, keep them inside, and cause them to tune out people around them.
- They get players outside running around and immersing themselves in their surroundings.
- They build competency in real-world navigation and social skills.

Parent Spying Apps

Parent spying apps enable parents to follow where their mobile phone-carrying children are at any time on a Web-based map. Some even enable parents to define a safe zone for their children, and they will send the parent an e-mail or text message if the children go outside this zone. Many mobile phone companies offer these apps as part of their service package, but other companies such as Disney also offer apps in this category.

These apps don't enable children to have more fun, nor do they enhance children's abilities to navigate. To them, these apps are invisible. Instead, they are for parents who want to keep track of their children.

Philosophically, I have a problem with parents spying on their children because it limits their children's freedom. However, parents who don't allow their children to leave the house alone are limiting their children's freedom even more.

I can imagine parents who would only allow their children to venture outside alone if they could track their children via one of these apps. For these parents, a parent spying app can be a short-term solution, but I'd hope they'd stop using them the moment they feel somewhat comfortable letting their children roam independently. For parents who aren't sure, I'd advise avoiding these apps entirely, letting their children roam with some clear rules (don't go beyond these boundaries, only go to this place, call me at 5 p.m., be home at 8 p.m.). If children are ever going to learn how to be independent and responsible, parents have to afford them some trust and hope that they follow the rules.

Playborhood as a Cultural Movement

Throughout this book, I encourage parents to think and act locally, even hyper-locally. To create a culture of neighborhood play for our children, we parents need to focus our attention on our immediate neighborhoods—i.e. our blocks—and our families.

However, it's undeniable that mass culture has a strong impact on our ability to change our local culture. Most of us work outside our immediate neighborhood, and all of us consume large amounts of mass media from disparate sources every day. We have phone conversations and e-mail exchanges with friends and relatives outside our neighborhoods every day. All of these outside forces strongly influence our thinking about how we raise our kids.

We simply can't ignore our friend who boasts about her child's accomplishments in myriad structured after-school activities, nor can we ignore all the books, television shows, and movies that practically never show children playing in their neighborhoods. The subtle yet constant messages we get from these sources construct a cultural image in our minds of a "normal" childhood.

In addition, child abductions get disproportionate attention in the media. Whether or not we choose to ignore this, our neighbors do not. Understandably, neighbor parents get freaked out and fearful, and that leads them to restrict their children's freedom. Their children suffer, and ours do as well.

Since I started blogging at Playborhood.com in 2007, I've encountered thousands of parents who would love to provide their children with a Playborhood. Of course, they need not only ideas on what steps to take, which this book provides, but they also thirst for some sort of validation from the broader culture that creating a Playborhood isn't some strange, quixotic quest. In other words, they need our culture to accept, and even embrace, neighborhood play as an integral part of childhood.

I'm on a mission to spread a "Playborhood cultural movement." Publishing this book is my largest effort yet in this mission, but I also blog regularly at Playborhood.com, speak to parent groups frequently, and appear on television and radio.

Numerous other activists are pushing in more or less the same direction, trying to rescue children's play. Like me, they blog and tweet, write articles and books, post on Facebook, and appear in the media.

Below is a listing of the movements to rescue children's play, along with a leading voice of each movement:

- **Neighborhoods and Free Play:** Mike Lanza, author of Playborhood (playborhood.com)
- **Children and Nature:** Richard Louv, author of *The Last Child in the Woods* and his Children and Nature Network (childrenandnature.org); landscape designers who advocate natural playscapes such as Tony Malkusak and Rusty Keeler (earthplay.net)
- **Overcoming Parental Fears:** Lenore Skenazy, author of *Free Range Kids* and her Free Range Kids blog (freerangekids.wordpress.com)
- **Play-Based, Progressive Curricula in Schools:** The Alliance for Childhood (allianceforchildhood.org), Waldorf Schools (whywaldorfworks.org)
- **School Recess:** Playworks (playworks.org)
- **Child Obesity:** First lady Michelle Obama's Let's Move campaign (letsmove.gov), the Robert Wood Johnson Foundation (rwjf.org/childhoodobesity)
- **Playgrounds for all Kids:** Kaboom! (kaboom.org)

These movements are all allied, albeit imperfectly. Many of us read each other's writings and cheer each other on. Besides the word "play," what all these movements have in common is a deep concern about the quality of children's lives today. We are concerned about the dominant cultural attitude toward childhood, as articulated to the extreme by the recent best-seller *The Battle Hymn of the Tiger Mother* by Amy Chua, which is that children should be forced to aim for success at all costs. In other words, childhood is nothing more than a preparatory phase for the drudgery of competitive adult life.

Those of us in the movements listed above disagree with the Tiger Mom. We believe that childhood should be about play and happiness, and that the pursuit of these today does not diminish from success later in life. In fact, there is a lot of evidence that play in childhood leads to academic success in high school and career success in the adult years.

The evidence from many sources indicates that children today aren't thriving compared to children of decades ago. They're far more likely to be depressed and obese. Smothered by adult authority, they perceive that they have less control over their lives, they're less creative, and they're less self-reliant. They lack purpose. These problems accumulate, so that when they reach their 20s, they're far less prepared for adult life.

As a father of three little boys, these facts make my blood boil. If you're still reading at this point, your blood's boiling, too.

Good. I want you to help my Playborhood movement or the other movements listed above to help change childhood in the 21st century. I want you to recommend this book to everyone you can. I want you to read books from the other movements like *The Last Child in the Woods* and *Free Range Kids*, and I want you to tell others to read those, too.

When any of us comes to speak to your community organization or school, I want you to attend, and I want you to convince your friends to come, too. On the Internet, I want you to tweet and comment and post on Facebook about our movements. I ask you to follow @playborhood on Twitter and retweet articles; visit Playborhood. com and comment on articles there; and like the Playborhood Facebook page and share its wall posts.

But most of all, I want you to make your own neighborhood vibrant and nurturing. I want you to build a neighborhood hangout in your front yard, play out there with your kids every evening, and then give them the tools they need to be independent of you. I want you to encourage your neighbors to join you.

In short, I want you to join the movement, or start your own movement, with the goal of promoting play and enhancing the quality of children's lives today. With enough voices, at a high enough volume, we can transform our culture's conception of what a "normal childhood" looks like.

So when a friend brags to you about her daughter's after-school Mandarin immersion program, you could counter by describing how your kids are building a tree house in the vacant lot next door. When another friend complains about a weekend packed with shuttling his kids to soccer games all over town, you can tell him about your delightful weekend in your own yard, puttering in the garden while watching your kids add a second floor. You'll realize that the Playborhood movement has potential if your friends act a tad jealous, wanting to know more about that tree house. You'll know that the Playborhood movement is actually catching on if they forget about the wonders of Mandarin and organized soccer, and instead strategize with you about creating a great neighborhood life for their kids.

Boy, that would be nice, wouldn't it?

Notes

Chapter 1

1. "Lifetime Prevalence of Mental Disorders in U.S. Adolescents: Results from the National Comorbidity Survey Replication—Adolescent Supplement (NCS-A)," by Kathleen Ries Merikangas, et al., *Journal of the American Academy of Child & Adolescent Psychiatry*, vol. 49, no. 10, October 2010, p. 980.
2. *The Lonely Crowd, Revised Edition. A Study of the Changing American Character*, by David Riesman with Rehuel Denney and Nathan Glazer, New Haven, Conn.: Yale University Press, 2001.
3. "The Organization Kid," by David Brooks, *The Atlantic*, April 2001. Accessed online on Jan. 17, 2012, at http://www.theatlantic.com/magazine/archive/2001/04/the-organization-kid/2164.
4. "The Decline of Play and the Rise of Psychopathology in Children and Adolescents," by Peter Gray, *American Journal of Play*, vol. 3, no. 4, 2011, p. 454.
5. *Flow: The Psychology of Optimal Experience*, by Mihaly Csikszentmihalyi, New York: Harper & Row, 1990.
6. Ibid., p. 443.
7. "Lifetime Prevalence of Mental Disorders," p. 980.
8. See "Mental Health of College Students and Their Non-College-Attending Peers," by Carlos Blanco, MD, PhD, et al., *Archives of General Psychiatry*, vol. 65, no. 12, December 2008, pp. 1,429–37.
9. "National Survey of Counseling Center Directors 2008," by Robert P. Gallagher, The International Association of Counseling Services Inc. Accessed online on Jan. 17, 2012, at http://www.iacsinc.org/2008%20National%20Survey%20of%20Counseling%20Center%20Directors.pdf.
10. *The Path to Purpose*, by William Damon, New York: Free Press, 2008, p. 8.
11. See, for example, *A Nation of Wimps: The High Cost of Invasive Parenting*, by Hara Estroff Marano, New York: Broadway, 2008; *The Last Child in the Woods: Saving Our Children from Nature-Deficit Disorder*, by Richard Louv, New York: Algonquin Books, 2008; *Parenting Without Fear: Letting Go of Worry and Focusing on What Really Matters*, by Paul J.

Donahue, New York: St. Martin's Griffin, 2007; and *The Price of Privilege: How Parental Pressure and Material Advantage Are Creating a Generation of Disconnected and Unhappy Kids*, by Madeline Levine, New York: Harper Paperbacks, 2008.

12. Data for child abductions comes from the National Criminal Justice Service (http://www. ncjrs.gov/html/ojjdp/nismart/qa/index.html). Data for automobile accidents comes from the *National Highway Traffic Safety Administration's Traffic Safety Facts 2008* (accessed online on Jan. 17, 2012, at http://www-nrd.nhtsa.dot.gov/pubs/811172.pdf). Don't spend too much time scrutinizing these data or their sources. The numbers are so out of proportion that they're not worth spending time on them.

13. The FBI's *Uniform Crime Reports* (http://www.fbi.gov/about-us/cjis/ucr/ucr) show that violent crime in the United States increased through the 1960s, '70s, and '80s, peaked in 1991, and decreased from then through today. The rate for 2010 was about at the same level as 1972. Most parents of young children today weren't even born in 1972.

14. *Free-Range Kids, How to Raise Safe, Self-Reliant Children (Without Going Nuts with Worry)*, by Lenore Skenazy, New York: Jossey-Bass, 2009.

15. This is a fundamental lesson of game theory, a branch of economics.

Chapter 2

1. The sources for most of the statistics cited in this chapter on children's use of time are the following two articles that document Sandra Hofferth's work in this area. Note that Hofferth has had various colleagues working with her over the years, such as John Sandberg, who is cited in the first article below, but I refer to these studies simply as the Hofferth studies for brevity. "Changes in American Children's Use of Time, 1981–97," by Sandra Hofferth and John Sandberg, in *Children at the Millennium: Where Have We Come From, Where Are We Going?*, New York: Elsevier Science, 2001, pp. 193–229; and "Changes in American Children's Time, 1997–2003," by Sandra Hofferth, *International Journal of Time Use Research*, vol. 6, no. 1, 2009, pp. 31–32. Accessed online on Jan. 17, 2012, at http://www.popcenter.umd.edu/search?SearchableText=Sandra+Hofferth

2. "The Rug Rat Race," by Garey Ramey and Valerie Ramey, Cambridge, Mass.: The National Bureau of Economic Research, 2009. Accessed online on Jan. 17, 2012, at http://www. econ.ucsd.edu/~vramey/research/Rugrat.pdf

3. "Generation M2: Media in the Lives of 8- to 18-Year-Olds," by the Kaiser Family Foundation, 2010. Accessed online on Jan. 17, 2012, at http://www.kff.org/entmedia/mh012010pkg. cfm

4. "Electronic media" is defined here as TV, the Internet, cell phones, video games, music and other audio, and movies. Also, note that not all electronic media consumption is in front of a screen. Listening to a portable music device and talking on a mobile phone do not require this. However, almost all the time children spend consuming electronic media in the Kaiser Family Foundation study is in front of screens, so I will use the terms "electronic media consumption" and "screen time" interchangeably in this book.

5. "Television and DVD/Video Viewing in Children Younger Than 2 Years," by Frederick Zimmerman, et al., *Archives of Pediatric and Adolescent Medicine*, vol. 161, no. 5, pp.

473–79. Accessed online on Jan. 17, 2012, at http://kidshealth.org/parent/positive/family/tv_affects_child.html

6. "TV Viewing Among Kids at an Eight-Year High," The Nielsen Company, 2009. Accessed online on Jan. 17, 2012, at http://blog.nielsen.com/nielsenwire/media_entertainment/tv-viewing-among-kids-at-an-eight-year-high

7. *Brand Child : Remarkable Insights into the Minds of Today's Global Kids & Their Relationships with Brands*, by Martin Lindstrom with Patricia Seybold, London: Kogan Page, 2003.

8. Ibid., p. 277.

Chapter 3

1. See the 2010 *U.S. News & World Report* "America's Best High Schools: Gold Medal List." Accessed online on Jan. 17, 2012, at http://education.usnews.rankingsandreviews.com/best-high-schools/rankings/gold-medal-list

2. The whiteboard material I used is "Dry Erase-Plus" (see http://dryeraseplus.com).

3. The American Academy of Orthopaedic Surgeons recommends in-ground trampolines for safety. See http://www.aaos.org/about/papers/position/1135.asp (accessed online on Jan. 17, 2012).

4. *The Big Orange Splot*, by Daniel Pinkwater, New York: Scholastic Paperbacks, 1993.

5. *Roxaboxen*, by Alice McLerran, New York: Harper Collins, 2004.

Chapter 4

1. "South Bronx Is America's Poorest District," by Josh Duboff, New York, Sept. 29, 2010. Accessed online on Jan. 17, 2012, at http://nymag.com/daily/intel/2010/09/south_bronx_is_americas_poores.html

2. "Activist's Mission Building: Says She Rescued It, but Price Is Too High," by Ralph R. Ortega, *The New York Daily News*, June 8, 2000.

3. This and many other quotes from Hetty Fox, unless noted otherwise, are from interviews by the author of Hetty Fox on Nov. 4 and 8, 2010.

4. "About New York; 'The Professor' is Keeping Lyman Place Alive," by William E. Geist, *The New York Times*, Nov. 3, 1984.

5. "Play Street Becomes a Sanctuary," by David Gonzalez, in *The New York Times*, July 31, 2009, accessed online on January 20, 2012, at http://www.nytimes.com/2009/08/02/nyregion/02ritual.html

6. "Play Street," Audio Slide Show, produced by Michael Kolomatsky, *The New York Times*. Accessed online on Jan. 17, 2012, at http://www.nytimes.com/interactive/2009/08/02/nyregion/20090802_playstreet_audio/index.html

7. "Activist Loses Her 'Home,'" by Jonalys Almanzar and Myles Miller, *The New York Daily News*, July 31, 2007.

8. "Play Street."

Chapter 5

1. "Building the World We Want: Interview with Mark Lakeman," by Brooke Jarvis, *Yes! Magazine*, May 12, 2010. Accessed online on Jan. 17, 2012, at http://www.yesmagazine. org/happiness/building-the-world-we-want-interview-with-mark-lakeman
2. "City Repair: Portland Residents Create Community Through Green Building," by Toby Hemenway, in *Natural Home and Garden*, January/February 2003. Accessed online on Jan. 17, 2012, at http://www.naturalhomeandgarden.com/Homes/2003-01-01/BENDING-THE-GRID.aspx

Chapter 6

1. I'll use "The Waters" to refer to just Lucas Point throughout the rest of this chapter.
2. *Suburban Nation: The Rise of Sprawl and the Decline of the American Dream*, by Andres Duany, et al., New York: North Point Press, 2000, p. 47.

Chapter 8

1. I got some aspects of this story about Lucy from "A Village That Loves Lucy," by Stephen Maganini, *The Sacramento Bee*, Nov. 25, 2010, page 1A.

Chapter 10

1. "Who's Minding the Kids? Child Care Arrangements: Spring 2005/Summer 2006," *Current Population Reports*, U.S. Census Bureau, by Lynda Laughlin. Accessed online on Jan. 17, 2012, at http://www.census.gov/prod/2010pubs/p70-121.pdf
2. Even though the Iris Way neighborhood encompasses one smaller street, Primrose Way, I'll just refer to the entire neighborhood as "Iris Way."

Chapter 11

1. According to U.S. Census data, 17.6 percent of children between the ages of 1 and 9 moved in a one-year period from 2006 to 2007. Data were accessed online on Jan. 17, 2012, in Excel format at http://www.census.gov/population/socdemo/migration/cps2007/tab07-01.xls
2. Accessed online on Jan. 17, 2012, at http://dictionary.reference.com/browse/neighborhood
3. *Livable Streets*, by Donald Appleyard, Berkeley, Calif.: University of California Press, 1981, pp. 15–24.
4. "Daily School Recess Improves Classroom Behavior," *ScienceDaily*. Accessed online on Jan. 17, 2012, at http://www.sciencedaily.com/releases/2009/01/090126173835.htm
5. For a discussion of how schools are restricting recess, see "School Recess Gets Gentler, and Adults Are Dismayed," *The New York Times*, Dec. 14, 2007, by Alison Leigh Cowan. Accessed online on Jan. 17, 2012, at http://www.nytimes.com/2007/12/14/

education/14recess.html?_r=1&ex=1198299600&en=6e0e6d84ce1d8305&ei=5070&emc=eta1

6. See *The Battle Over Homework*, by Harris Cooper, New York: Corwin Press, 2006. Note that, despite the fact that Cooper states that there is no conclusive evidence that homework results in academic achievement for elementary school students, he recommends that they be given 10 minutes of homework per night for every grade level — i.e., 10 minutes per night for first graders, 20 minutes per night for second graders, etc. Obviously, Cooper's recommendation is not consistent with his research results.

7. The school's name is Oak Knoll Elementary School, the principal is David Ackerman, and you can read about his reduced homework policy at http://www.almanacnews.com/news/show_story.php?id=436 (accessed online on Jan. 17, 2012).

8. The sample for this survey is far from scientific, but I still believe in the general validity of the results. See http://playborhood.com/2007/11/playborhood_survey_iii_parents_are_willing_to_pay_for_play (accessed online on Jan. 17, 2012).

9. America's Fair Housing laws, of which the Fair Housing Act is the most significant, are designed to prohibit discrimination in all activities associated with the rental and purchase of homes. For more information, see http://www.hud.gov/offices/fheo/FHLaws (accessed online on Jan. 17, 2012).

10. "Questions Your Realtor Can't Answer," by Vivian S. Toy, *The New York Times*, June 24, 2007. Accessed online on Jan. 17, 2012, at http://www.nytimes.com/2007/06/24/realestate/24cov.html

11. One notable exception to this rule is New York City, which, interestingly, also is the only major real estate market without a multi-list service, according to: "How Fair Housing Laws Affect Realtors' Ability to Market to Families with Children," by Relman and Dane LLP, unpublished working paper, 2009.

12. Swinging in Place: Porch Life in Southern Culture, by Jocelyn Hazelwood Donlon, Chapel Hill, N.C.: The University of North Carolina Press, 2001.

13. From Front Porch to Back Seat: Courtship in Twentieth-Century America, by Beth L. Bailey, Baltimore: Johns Hopkins University Press, 1988.

14. These "front porch campaigns" are well documented in The American Porch: An Informal History of an Informal Place, by Michael Dolan, Guilford, Conn.: The Lyons Press, 2002.

15. See, for example, *Swinging in Place*.

16. Although there's no hard data on the percent of houses built with porches before 1992, anecdotal evidence from homebuilders suggests that they practically died out in the 1960s and '70s. In 1992, the U.S. Census states that 42 percent of all new houses had a porch, and that this number increased to 58 percent in 2007. The National Association of Homebuilders reports that its members expect that number to eclipse 70 percent by 2015. See http://www.ohio.com/news/top-stories/step-right-up-1.140331 (accessed online on Jan. 17, 2012).

Chapter 12

1. You can view a video of me interviewing my dad about his childhood play memories at http://www.youtube.com/watch?v=qnXtDnCfMNM.
2. "Why Youth (Heart) Social Networking Sites: The Role of Networked Publics in Teenage Social Life," by Danah Boyd, in *Youth, Identity, and Digital Media*, Cambridge, Mass.: The MIT Press, 2008, p. 134.
3. Ibid., p. 137.
4. "How children lost the right to roam in four generations," by David Derbyshire, *The Daily Mail*, June 15, 2007. Accessed online on Jan. 17, 2012, at http://www.dailymail.co.uk/news/article-462091/How-children-lost-right-roam-generations.html#ixzz0yxrQfz3o
5. A well-known advocate of parks as solutions to the problem of children's lack of outdoor play is Kaboom.org (see http://kaboom.org).
6. "The Special Value of Children's Age-Mixed Play," by Peter Gray, in *American Journal of Play*, vol. 3, no. 4, 2011. Accessed online at http://www.journalofplay.org/sites/www.journalofplay.org/files/pdf-articles/3-4-article-gray-age-mixed-play.pdf
7. This affection for backyards is rather recent in American history. In the first half of the 20th century and before, backyards were unsightly and putrid. In these days before indoor plumbing and automobiles, outhouses and horse stables were behind the house. The front porch was the more pristine social space.
8. "Another backyard rink in the books," by John Buccigross, ESPN.com, Jan. 21, 2009. Accessed online on Jan. 17, 2012, at http://sports.espn.go.com/nhl/columns/story?columnist=buccigross_john&id=3846952

Chapter 13

1. *Your Brain on Childhood: The Unexpected Side Effects of Classrooms, Ballparks, Family Rooms, and the Minivan*, by Gabrielle Principe, Amherst, N.Y.: Prometheus Books, 2011, p. 13.
2. Ibid., p. 24.
3. "Children, Adolescents, and Television," Washington, D.C.: American Academy of Pediatrics, 2001. Accessed online on Jan. 17, 2012, at http://aappolicy.aappublications.org/cgi/reprint/pediatrics;107/2/423
4. "Resurrecting Free Play in Young Children: Looking Beyond Fitness and Fatness to Attention, Affiliation, and Affect," by Hillary L. Burdette, MD, MS; and Robert C. Whitaker, MD, MPH, *Archives of Pediatrics & Adolescent Medicine*, vol. 159, January 2005, pp. 46-50. Accessed online on Jan. 17, 2012, at http://www.childrenandnature.org/downloads/Burdette_LookingBeyond.pdf
5. "The Magic of the Family Meal," by Nancy Gibbs, *Time*, June 4, 2006. Accessed online on Jan. 17, 2012, at http://www.time.com/time/magazine/article/0,9171,1200760,00.html
6. See *iBrain: Surviving the Technological Alteration of the Modern Mind*, by Gary Small and Gigi Vorgan, New York: Harper Paperbacks, 2009; and *The Shallows: What the Internet Is Doing to Our Brains*, by Nicholas Carr, New York: W.W. Norton & Co., 2010.

7. "Brain Development: How Much TV Should Children Watch?" by David Perlmutter, MD, *The Huffington Post*, Dec. 6, 2010. Accessed online on Jan. 17, 2012, at http://www.huffingtonpost.com/dr-david-perlmutter-md/television-and-the-develo_b_786934.html

8. "The Risks of Parenting While Plugged In," by Julie Scelfo, *The New York Times*, June 9, 2010. Accessed online on Jan. 17, 2012, at http://www.nytimes.com/2010/06/10/garden/10childtech.html

9. "Summary of Travel Trends: 2001 National Household Travel Survey," Federal Highway Administration, Washington, D.C.: U.S. Department of Transportation, 2004, p. 28. Accessed online on Jan. 17, 2012, at http://nhts.ornl.gov/2001/pub/STT.pdf

10. "Child Passenger Safety: Fact Sheet," Atlanta: Centers of Disease Control and Prevention, 2010. Accessed online on Jan. 17, 2012, at http://www.cdc.gov/motorvehiclesafety/child_passenger_safety/cps-factsheet.html

11. "Travel and Environmental Implications of School Siting," U.S. Environmental Protection Agency, EPA231-R-03-004, October 2003. Accessed online on Jan. 17, 2012, at http://www.epa.gov/smartgrowth/pdf/school_travel.pdf

12. "The Effect of Dramatic Play on Children's Generation of Cohesive Text," by Anthony Pellegrini, *Discourse Processes*, vol. 7, no. 1, 1984, pp. 57–67, as cited in *Your Brain on Childhood*.

13. "Children's Independent Movement in the Local Environment," by Roger Mackett, et al., *Built Environment*, vol. 33, no. 4, December 2007, pp. 454–68, as cited in *Your Brain on Childhood*, by Principe.

14. "The Magic of the Family Meal."

15. See *The Irish Storyteller*, by Georges Denis Zimmermann, Dublin: Four Courts Press, 2001.

16. A great book about how to structure good stories is *Story: Substance, Structure, Style, and the Principles of Screenwriting*, by Robert McKee, New York: Harper Entertainment, 1997.

17. *The Raft*, by Jim LaMarche, New York: HarperCollins, 2002.

18. *Weslandia*, by Paul Fleischman, Somerville, Mass.: Candlewick Press, 2002.

19. *The Busy Life of Ernestine Buckmeister*, by Linda Lodding, Brooklyn, N.Y.: Flashlight Press, 2011.

Chapter 14

1. *It Takes a Village, Tenth Anniversary Edition*, by Hillary Rodham Clinton, New York: Simon & Schuster, 2006.

2. "Neighborhood Context, Poverty, and Urban Children's Outdoor Play," by Rachel Tolbert Kimbro, et al., Fragile Families Working Paper: WP10-04-FF. Accessed online on Jan. 17, 2012, at http://crcw.princeton.edu/workingpapers/WP10-04-FF.pdf

3. A children playing sign with the Playborhood logo is available for sale. See Playborhood.com for details.

4. *Parenting Without Fear*, pp. 275–78.

Chapter 15

1. One notable book on this topic that focuses on the particular problems of twentysome-thing males is *Manning Up: How the Rise of Women Has Turned Men into Boys*, by Kay Hymowitz, New York: Basic Books, 2011. A seminal magazine article on the topic is "What Is It About 20-Somethings?" by Robin Marantz Henig, *The New York Times Magazine*, Aug. 18, 2010. Accessed online on Jan. 17, 2012, at http://www.nytimes.com/2010/08/22/magazine/22Adulthood-t.html

2. *Lost in Transition: The Dark Side of Emerging Adulthood*, by Christian Smith, et al., New York: Oxford University Press, 2011.

3. *Drive: The Surprising Truth About What Motivates Us*, by Daniel H. Pink, New York: Riverhead Books, 2009.

4. Ibid., p. 131.

5. "Children's Autonomy and Responsibility: An Analysis of Childrearing Advice," by Markella Rutherford, *Qualitative Sociology*, vol. 32, 2009, pp. 340.

6. *1969 National Personal Transportation Survey: Travel to School*, Federal Highway Administration, Washington, D.C.: U.S. Department of Transportation; 1972. Accessed online on Jan. 17, 2012, at http://www.fhwa.dot.gov/ohim/1969/q.pdf

7. *Travel and Environmental Implications of School Siting*, U.S. Environmental Protection Agency, Washington, D.C.: U.S. Environmental Protection Agency, 2003. Accessed online on Jan. 17, 2012, at http://www.epa.gov/smartgrowth/pdf/school_travel.pdf

8. "The Amazing Collapse of the Working Teen," by Joe Weisenthal, *Business Insider*, Jan. 9, 2011. Accessed online on Jan. 17, 2012, at http://www.businessinsider.com/teen-unemployment-2011-1

9. These data were pieced together from two studies by Sandra Hofferth. The first is "Changes in American Children's Time, 1981–1997," by Sandra Hofferth and John Sandberg, in *Children at the Millennium: Where Have We Come From, Where Are We Going? Advances in Life Course Research*, New York: Elsevier Science, 2001. The second is "Changes in American Children's Time, 1997–2003," by Sandra Hofferth, *International Journal of Time Use Research*, vol. 6, no. 1, 2009: 26–47.

10. "Survey: 43% of Parents Have Done Kids' Homework," *Los Angeles Times* blogs. Accessed online on Jan. 17, 2012, at http://latimesblogs.latimes.com/thehomeroom/2008/08/its-9-pm-and-th.html

11. *The Price of Privilege*, p. 70.

12. "The Rug Rat Race."

13. "Parents and Kids See Quality Time Differently—Families." Accessed online on Jan. 17, 2012, at http://findarticles.com/p/articles/mi_m1272/is_2691_131/ai_95449607

14. *The Philosophical Baby : What Children's Minds Tell Us About Truth, Love, and the Meaning of Life*, by Alison Gopnik, New York: Picador, 2010.

15. For example, see "All Joy and No Fun: Why Parents Hate Parenting," *New York Magazine*, July 4, 2010. Accessed online on Jan. 17, 2012, at http://nymag.com/print/?/news/features/67024

16. *The Moral Judgment of the Child*, by Jean Piaget, New York: Free Press, 1997.

17. See two literature reviews of the effects of nature on children: "Is Contact with Nature Important for Healthy Child Development? State of the Evidence," by Andrea Faber Taylor and Frances E. Kuo, *Children and Their Environments: Learning, Using, and Designing Spaces*, Cambridge, U.K.: Cambridge University Press, 2006; and "Children in the Outdoors: A Literature Review," by S.A. Muñoz, Sustainable Development Research Centre (accessed online on Jan. 17, 2012, at http://www.apho.org.uk/resource/view.aspx?RID=93474).

Chapter 16

1. *An American Childhood*, by Annie Dillard. New York: Perennial Library, 1988, p. 43.
2. *The Life and Times of the Thunderbolt Kid: A Memoir*, by Bill Bryson, New York: Boradway, 2007, p. 220.
3. *Teens and Mobile Phones*, by the Pew Internet and American Life Project, April 2010, pp. 112–13. Accessed online on Jan. 17, 2012, at http://www.pewinternet.org/Reports/2010/Teens-and-Mobile-Phones.aspx
4. *Ibid.*, p. 8.
5. *Networked Families*, by the Pew Internet and American Life Project, October 2008, p. 35. Accessed online on Jan. 17, 2012, at http://www.pewinternet.org/Reports/2008/Networked-Families.aspx
6. *Networked Families*, p. 36.
7. *Teens and Mobile Phones*, p. 25.
8. See Mobi-Kids, accessed online on Jan. 17, 2012, at http://www.mbkds.com
9. "Study Finds Teens' Late Night Media Use Comes at a Price" by Ellin Holohan, *U.S. News & World Report*, Nov. 1, 2010. Accessed online on Jan. 17, 2012, at http://health.usnews.com/health-news/family-health/brain-and-behavior/articles/2010/11/01/study-finds-teens-late-night-media-use-comes-at-a-price.html
10. *Teens and Mobile Phones*, p. 149.
11. "New Data from Virginia Tech Transportation Institute Provides Insight into Cell Phone Use and Driving Distraction." Accessed online on Jan. 17, 2012, at http://www.vtnews.vt.edu/articles/2009/07/2009-571.html

Index

MIKE LANZA has been blogging at Playborhood.com on the subject of children's play in neighborhoods since 2007. This book follows on that work. He resides in Menlo Park, California, with his wife, Perla Ni, and their three boys, Marco, Nico, and Leo. Prior to his writing career, Mike was a five-time software and Internet entrepreneur in Silicon Valley. He holds an MA in Education, an MBA, and an MA and BA in Economics, all from Stanford University. Way back, in the 1960s and 70s, he spent a splendid childhood laughing, running, and thinking in the suburbs of Pittsburgh, PA.

14667586R00135

Made in the USA
Lexington, KY
12 April 2012